Jennifer Fulwiler takes us on the  to balance work and family duties in a _____ uffaw, cringe, and ultimately walk awa_____ r own dreams in *One Beautiful Dream*.

_____ *es* best-
selling author and broadcaster

When I finished reading the very last line of *One Beautiful Dream*, I applauded. What a treat this book is! And if you've ever struggled with wanting to give family life everything you have but wondering how your God-given passions fit in with that, you're going to be so encouraged by Jen's story. There is so much grace in these pages, so many accounts of how creatively the Lord cares and provides for us as we work out our callings with our families. *One Beautiful Dream* is hilarious, life-giving, and tender—an all-the-way-real reminder that sometimes, when life looks nothing like we expected, it's so much better than we could have ever imagined.

SOPHIE HUDSON, author of *Giddy Up, Eunice*
and cohost of *The Big Boo Cast*

I believe the family is the center of everything, but for those of us fighting the battle to hold ours together, the first casualty is often ourselves. *One Beautiful Dream* is a must-read for everyone who is pouring their whole heart and love into nurturing their children while struggling to maintain their own creativity and identity. You really can "have it all," but it just may not be the way you expect. Jennifer Fulwiler's funny, poignant, and oh-so-personal writing style makes reading this book like a fantastic conversation with a dear friend. You will find yourself crying and laughing along with this epic journey of personal discovery.

JEANNIE GAFFIGAN, executive producer, head
writer, *The Jim Gaffigan Show*

All we need to do is be who God made us to be. That's an arduous joy, and Jennifer Fulwiler is honest and heartfelt and funny about it. The universal call to holiness looks different for each one of us—and is often something of a mess by worldly standards. Fulwiler is a tremendous friend to have on the journey. Jennifer Fulwiler—and this book—will help you and those you love. *One Beautiful Dream* will help you love with greater freedom, which, as Pope Francis has emphasized, is God's dream for us. Reading this book is an encounter with God's dream for you. You'll also laugh and cry with her and come to quickly love her and her family!

KATHRYN JEAN LOPEZ, senior fellow, The National Review
Institute and editor-at-large, *National Review*

Marvelous! This book will breathe life into so many hollowed parents who feel stuck between their families and side passions. Most of us wonder: How can we do both? How can we be devoted family people and live out our personal dreams? This refreshing memoir shows the way. It's not a fluffy self-help guide. The book is deliciously witty, insightful, absorbing, and offers one motivational epiphany after another, each punching a hole in the Resistance blocking us from our dreams. If every parent read this, families would become dream incubators, not where passions go dormant.

BRANDON VOGT, bestselling author and founder of ClaritasU

It would be enough to read *One Beautiful Dream* for its hilarity. Enough to read it for its brilliant insights and powerful writing. Enough to read it for the rollicking story of how Jen Fulwiler found her best self while losing herself under laundry for eight and diapers and the weight of an audacious dream. But when you combine it all, you'll find a breathtaking look at a modern family life built on ancient truths. Grab this book and devour it for the soul-satisfying nourishment it delivers.

JULIE LYLES CARR, author, *Raising an Original: Parenting
Each Child According to Their Unique God-Given
Temperament* and host of *The Modern Motherhood Podcast*

Jennifer Fulwiler is a great writer, plain and simple. And a deep thinker. Combine all that with a cutting sense of humor and you've got an immensely readable story. Oh, and it will change the way you think about family life forever. Other than that, this isn't much of a book.

PATRICK LENCIONI, best-selling author, *The Five Dysfunctions
of a Team* and *The Three Big Questions for a Frantic
Family*, and cofounder, The Amazing Parish

ONE
BEAUTIFUL
DREAM

ALSO BY JENNIFER FULWILER

*Something Other Than God: How I Passionately
Sought Happiness and Accidentally Found It*

The rollicking tale of family chaos,

ONE
BEAUTIFUL
DREAM

personal passions, and saying yes to them both

Jennifer Fulwiler

ZONDERVAN

ZONDERVAN

One Beautiful Dream
Copyright © 2018 by Jennifer Fulwiler

Requests for information should be addressed to:
Zondervan, *3900 Sparks Dr. SE, Grand Rapids, Michigan 49546*

ISBN 978–0–310–35203-7 (softcover)

ISBN 978–0–310–35312-6 (audio)

ISBN 978–0–310–34975–4 (ebook)

Library of Congress Cataloging-in-Publication Data

Names: Fulwiler, Jennifer, author.
Title: One beautiful dream : the rollicking tale of family chaos, personal passions, and
   saying yes to them both / Jennifer Fulwiler.
Description: Grand Rapids, Michigan : Zondervan, [2018]
Identifiers: LCCN 2017047724 | ISBN 9780310349747 (hardcover)
Subjects: LCSH: Motherhood. | Parenting.
Classification: LCC HQ759 .F84 2018 | DDC 248.8/431—dc23 LC record available at
   https://lccn.loc.gov/2017047724

The author is represented by Alive Literary Agency, 7680 Goddard Street, Suite 200,
Colorado Springs, Colorado 80920, www.aliveliterary.com.

Art direction: Curt Diepenhorst
Interior design: Denise Froehlich

Printed in the United States of America

19 20 21 22 23 24 25 /LSC/ 10 9 8 7 6 5 4 3 2 1

For Joe, Donnell, Lane, Lucy,
Kate, Pammy, and JT.
You are my one beautiful dream.

Contents

Foreword by Melanie Shankle 11
Introduction 13

1. POSSUMGATE 15
2. BLUE FLAME 22
3. AT LEAST WE HAVE QUESO 28
4. FAMILY PLANNING (AND OTHER THINGS I'M NOT GOOD AT) 33
5. BEER BONG PLAYDATE 40
6. VIRAL 44
7. LOAVES OF BREAD 46
8. A FRIENDSHIP IS BORN 50
9. SHOT IN THE DARK 56
10. WHOLENESS OF VISION 60
11. FOR THE LOVE OF THE BLOB 67
12. THE REPLY 74
13. THE OFFICE 78
14. HOUSTON, WE HAVE A PROBLEM 83
15. BFFS 89
16. NO FREAKING OUT 96
17. THE FARMER'S WIFE 103
18. POOPOCALYPSE 110
19. IF YOU'RE HAPPY AND YOU KNOW IT 117
20. BIBLE CHARADES 123
21. TEX-MEX EPIPHANY 131
22. BANANA MAN 137
23. FAMILY MEETING 144
24. A BEAUTIFUL HOME 148
25. ADVENT ROCK 154

26. RESISTANCE 161
27. DECIBEL 168
28. LIFE PARTY 173
29. HOTEL ROOM SHUFFLE 180
30. BREATHLESS 186
31. RUNNING UNDER WATER 190
32. LIFTED UP 196
33. "THAT COULD HAVE BEEN ME" 202
34. THE DRIVE 209
35. THE NIGHT WATCH 216
36. MY REAL LIFE 222
37. THE BOX 227
38. RELEASE 230

Acknowledgments 236

Foreword

I FIRST MET JEN FULWILER at a small Mexican restaurant in San Marcos, Texas, in 2007. We had read each other's blogs and kind of gotten to know each other through a series of emails, but this was back when it still felt a little weird to go meet someone in person you only knew through the internet. I convinced myself it would be okay because she was a devout Christian and I believed that her faith probably didn't go hand in hand with being a serial killer. Fortunately, this turned out to be true.

But what struck me about Jen that first day at lunch was how intelligent she is about so many things. She'd be the first to laugh and roll her eyes and make a sarcastic comment about this, but it's true. She is smart and witty, which are two characteristics that rank high on my imaginary priority list of what I like in a friend. We talked much longer than I planned for at lunch that day about everything from blog algorithms and coding (she talked; I listened because...what?) to our families, our faith, and our hopes and dreams. And I walked away that day knowing that I'd just experienced an online friendship becoming a real life friendship because I adored Jen Fulwiler.

We have continued to meet for lunch somewhere between Austin and San Antonio a couple of times a year. Every time I see her, I'm struck again by what an unexpected gift she has been in my life. What are the odds that two self-proclaimed introverts would take the initiative to meet in real life and then continue to do so on a regular basis?

A huge part of our friendship for me is that Jen inspires me. Her story of transitioning from being an atheist to a Christian is unusual enough, but when you add in the part about a driven, ambitious woman who never really aspired to be a mother finding herself with six kids and yet still manages to pursue her dreams? Now that is someone I want in my life.

Here's the thing about Jen. She is real, she is raw, and she is funny. She isn't one to sugarcoat anything or try to make life seem like it's always magical and wonderful. She's the first to say that having six kids and being married and juggling a radio-and-writing career is at times exhausting and may occasionally cause her to lose her mind. She balances all these things, yet is the first to admit that maybe the reality is women can kind of sort of have it all as long as they don't mind doing it with a spit-up stain on their shoulder and a screaming toddler in the background.

Jen is a constant reminder to me that God has dreams for all of us that go so far beyond what we can imagine and most certainly take our lives in a direction that we never planned, but following him will never be boring. She's a picture of what God can do with a woman who will say yes even when it looks messy, even when it looks hard, and even when it's so different from the picture you had in your head. And as you read the pages of *One Beautiful Dream*, you will find yourself wishing you could meet her for Mexican food in a small little restaurant in San Marcos because once you get to know her, it's hard to get enough of Jen Fulwiler.

—MELANIE SHANKLE

Introduction

IMAGINE THAT WE ARE AT A DINNER PARTY. You've sat down next to me, and I smile and say hello—and then start to give you a one-armed hug but switch to a handshake because I'm really socially awkward.

We get to talking, and I ask you all about you: Where are you from? What are your favorite TV shows to binge watch? What is your greatest passion in life?

And then you ask me about my story. It comes out that I used to be a careerist atheist who never wanted a family, yet I ended up having six babies in eight years, and learned how to follow my dreams in the process. If, at that point, you were to ask me how that happened, I would tell you something like this...

Possumgate

"I DON'T WANT A POSSUM IN THE HOUSE!" A woman browsing canned green beans next to me glanced my direction, so I lowered my voice when I spoke into the phone. "Our house has a no-possum rule."

My mother-in-law was perplexed. "Since when?"

"Since you told me you caught a possum."

I could tell that this was going to turn into an involved conversation, which was not ideal timing considering that I was at the store with two young children. Donnell, my two-year-old, was already pleading for snacks. And Lane, my feisty, red-headed one-year-old began to twist and kick to get out of her seat in the front of the shopping cart. It was getting close to her nap time, and I was going to have to hurry if I wanted to finish this trip before she entered the dreaded pre-nap danger zone.

"This animal is going to have to stay back at your house when you come visit, okay?" I said, hoping in vain to bring a quick end to the conversation.

"Aren't you a frisky little thing!"

"What?"

"I'm talking to the possum. Anyway, Jennifer, you're the one who told me to catch him!"

What had actually happened is that my husband's mom, whom we call Yaya, mentioned that a possum was digging holes in her yard. I made a passing comment that my son, Donnell, would love to see that. In her zeal to delight him and his sister, she caught it and was planning to bring it on her upcoming visit to our house.

"Yaya, how do you know this animal doesn't have rabies?"

"You don't have rabies, do you?"

I was pretty sure that the Centers for Disease Control didn't consider *asking the animal* to be a valid rabies test, but I had more immediate concerns. Donnell had begun squirming to get out of his seat next to Lane, and he was knocking into her in protest. I had already tried to invoke the bogey man of the Store Manager, reminding him that "The Store Manager gets very mad when little boys get out of carts in his store!" Unfortunately, that threat had worn off. I compromised by allowing him to move to the main basket of the cart. I hoisted him into place, a process which was a lot easier when I was not in the third trimester of pregnancy.

Normally, I was not crazy enough to take both kids to the store by myself, especially not now that I was pregnant and exhausted. I was an only child who had no background with young children—I had a hard enough time dealing with my life when we were safely confined in our extremely childproofed home. But I'd decided to risk this trip because I had run out of heavy cream mid-recipe.

I was putting together a tomato bisque recipe I'd gotten from a trendy downtown restaurant back when I had the kind of life where I ate at trendy downtown restaurants. This would be the first time in months that my lunch did not consist of scraps from the kids' food, and my empty stomach rumbled when I anticipated that first savory spoonful. The onions and garlic were already sautéed, currently getting cold in a frying pan on my stove. I just needed to grab this cream and get a few other things on the list. Then I could escape back to my house, have the satisfaction of eating a home-cooked meal, and get everyone down for a long nap.

But I wasn't about to explain all that to Yaya.

"It is a three-hour drive from your house to ours. You really think it would work to have a possum riding shotgun with you the whole way?"

"Sure! Sounds like fun to me." Yaya grew up below the poverty line in east Texas, and I grew up in middle-class suburbs with decorative flower beds and Yard of the Month awards. We often had different ideas about what sounded like fun.

"I won't even let it out of the cage when it's in the kids' bedrooms," she continued.

"Their *bedrooms*?"

"Alright, don't get wound up. We can keep him in the living room if that's what you want."

I shuddered. "And have you thought of what we'll do with this possum once the kids have seen it?"

She hemmed and hawed in the tone of someone trying to find a polite answer to an irrelevant question. "Well, we could release it into that park by your house." Sensing my dissatisfaction, she thought some more. "I guess we could eat it."

"Eat the possum?!" I shouted.

The green beans woman shot me a startled look. She adjusted her designer gray jacket and turned away. I wasn't sure if Yaya was kidding or not, but now wasn't the time to find out.

"Look, Yaya, I'm at the store and have got to get back home to finish this recipe. Let's talk about this later." We exchanged friendly goodbyes, though when she said "love ya, darlin'" I still wasn't sure if she was talking to the possum or to me.

Just as I hung up, Lane decided that she, too, was tired of sitting at the front of the cart. She let out a few angry grunts that indicated that this grocery run was about to go downhill quickly. I handed her a small bag of jelly beans that I held in reserve for moments like this.

I thought of the vegetables sitting in a pan on my stove and picked up the pace. I wove through the aisles, grabbing items without stopping, moving like someone imitating a maniacal race car driver. Donnell completing the effect by gripping the sides of the cart and shouting, "*Vrooooom!*"

I swung around into the pasta aisle only to find someone standing right in my path. I yanked the cart to a halt just a foot short of hitting her. The force of the stop caused Donnell to fall over in the cart, his sound effects abruptly stopping with "*Vrooo*—"

The woman jumped back, and her face flashed anger before she regained her composure. I recognized the steel-gray blazer and the short-cropped black hair with elegant silver streaks. It was Green Bean Lady.

The sudden stop rattled Lane and she lost her grip on the bag of jelly beans, the colorful candies now bouncing across the floor at my feet. When the reality of her new, candy-less life sunk in, she erupted into a full force scream-cry.

"I'm so sorry," I stammered to the woman we'd almost hit. I dropped to my knees to scramble after the jelly beans on the floor.

Green Bean Lady took a moment to behold the mess in front of her. I noticed that her hand-held basket contained only a few neatly-placed items, and her skirt suit ensemble had that telltale sheen of a recent trip to the dry cleaners. It occurred to me then that I hadn't brushed my hair today. Also, I wished I'd put on something other than this old, faded t-shirt.

"My, don't you have your hands full." I could barely hear her over Lane. "And another one on the way!"

I knew where this was headed. The past few months had taught me an immutable truth of human behavior: when people see a pregnant woman with a two-year-old and a baby, they absolutely must talk to her about her family planning choices as well as their own.

"I remember having two little ones," she said—I think, it was really hard to hear her. "But we stopped after that. Two was enough for us!"

"Okay . . ." I demonstrated intense focus on my task of picking up the candies, hoping that my diligence would signal that there was no need for small talk.

"I had a hard enough time with only two. I knew I couldn't give my kids a good life if I had more. It would have been irresponsible, really."

Still on my hands and knees, I'd been reaching for a jelly bean that had bounced under the cart. I paused and looked up at her. For a split second our eyes met, though neither of us spoke. Suddenly I was acutely aware of the person she imagined me to be. As if a spotlight had clicked on and illuminated my hunched figure on the grocery store floor, I felt exposed. My maternity jeans were too tight and had visible stains on them—and, now that I thought about it, might be showing my underwear. I wore no makeup. My hair was months overdue for a trim. I had just turned 30, but I looked years older. There were dark circles under my eyes from the fatigue that comes with three pregnancies in short succession and children who don't always sleep through the night.

If I had had a picture of myself from five years before, I probably would have fished it out and showed it to her, saying, "*This* is who I am." She would have seen a young woman with a bright red dye job that matched the take-no-prisoners, defiant expression on her face. The lady might have even been impressed to hear that this girl was a programmer at a tech startup who had been promoted twice in the past year and now, at just three years out of college, was pulling in an impressive salary. Certainly this lady wouldn't have been surprised to hear that the girl in this picture said she didn't want to have children and didn't even care if she got married; she didn't have any natural maternal instincts and was thrilled at the thought of throwing herself into her career. But I didn't have such a picture on me, and I was left with the sinking realization that Green Bean Lady perceived that the woman who crouched before her was the real me.

I was jerked out of my thoughts when Donnell grabbed an eight-dollar box of gluten-free, organic Vietnamese rice spaghetti and swung it through the air like a sword. Lane simultaneously released a particularly startling shriek that left me unable to think about anything but possible eardrum damage. I hoisted myself to a standing position, tossing the bag of now-garbage jelly beans into the cart. I got Lane to take her pacifier and then set to work wrestling that spaghetti away from Donnell.

I expected Green Bean Lady to move on from this spectacle, but she remained in front of my cart. "So . . . I guess you're done after this one," she said, nodding toward my uterus.

I was pretty sure that she didn't want a twenty-minute answer in which I detailed my conflicting thoughts on this subject, so I just answered, "I don't know. We're definitely done for a while, but we'll see after that." I cut the conversation off by saying I had to go and swung the cart in the opposite direction. The pasta aisle had nothing to offer me that would make it worth continuing this discussion.

The moment I lurched the cart to the right was the same moment Donnell leaned over to the left to get that organic pasta back from the shelf. As if watching a slow-motion action sequence in a movie called *Worst Day Ever*, Donnell's feet left the cart as he fell forward. His legs flipped fully over his head, and he took out a few boxes of noodles on the shelves before landing on his bottom. Green Bean Lady's mouth was agape.

Donnell's wailing shrieks filled the entire store, all the way up to the distant ceiling of the cavernous, warehouse-sized building. After I determined that he was okay, I pulled him close. I grabbed onto the cart to lift my pregnant self up while holding a crying, flailing child. The noise and commotion further riled up Lane, who spit out her pacifier to join the screaming.

When I got to a standing position, I met eyes with Green Bean Lady. All of my embarrassment and frustration and deeply-buried questions about my own life choices collided like atoms in a nuclear reactor, and I projected the resulting explosion onto her. *Why did you have all these kids if you can't even take care of them?* her expression said to me. *Your kids are miserable. You're miserable. What are you doing with your life?*

Carrying my son on my hip and pushing the grocery cart with my free hand, I ran toward the checkout lane. I paid for the groceries in a blur (the checker skipped the part about asking me if I was having a nice day) and escaped into the parking lot.

A burst of hot air hit me as soon as I opened the door to the car, whose black exterior had spent the better part of an hour soaking in the heat from the blazing Texas sun. After getting the kids strapped into the seats, I flopped into the driver's seat. Just the exertion of getting from the store to the car left me panting and sweaty. I turned the ignition and started the air conditioner. And along with the first waves of cool air, the realization hit me:

The cream.

I forgot the cream. The only reason I'd even made this trip. The key ingredient to the tomato bisque, the creation of which would be my only tangible accomplishment this week. I'd forgotten it. My husband, Joe, was working late so he wouldn't have time to pick it up, and I definitely was not dragging these kids back into that store.

I noted that it's good that God didn't give me access to a big, red *BLOW UP WORLD NOW* button.

And then I burst into tears.

Both kids were still whimpering in the back seat, and now I joined in the little chorus of misery with my own sobs.

Maybe everything I'd read into that interaction with Green Bean Lady was right. Maybe I was ruining everyone's lives with my incompetence as a parent. My love for my kids was infinite. It was my life's greatest blessing to be their mother. But I wasn't happy. On the average day I found myself exhausted, my brain running in the red zone like a car about to overheat. All of my plans for fun stuff to do as a family never seemed to materialize amidst the chaos and grinding fatigue. All of my personal goals had been buried for so long that I was starting to forget what they were.

My phone rang, and I saw through tear-blurred vision that it was Joe. I grabbed a used fast food napkin from the floor to dry my eyes and wipe my nose. Then I answered the phone to hear him say:

"You're going to let Yaya bring the possum, right?"

Blue Flame

YAYA ARRIVED FRIDAY MORNING, sans possum. To everyone's disappointment but mine, she made the three-hour trip from Houston to Austin alone after the animal escaped back into her yard.

She showed up like a merry SWAT team, ringing the doorbell repeatedly while pounding the door with her fist and shouting for someone to let her in. I eased myself up from my position on the couch and waddled to the door. As soon as I opened it, Yaya blew into the house like a tornado of fun. In less than a minute she'd swooped the kids into her arms, left lipstick marks on their cheeks, and had all the lights and the television on. If we'd owned a disco ball and a strobe light, those would have been switched on, too.

Immediately she announced that it was time to potty train Donnell. I started to tell her about the five-step method that I found in a parenting book, but before I could finish she had dropped an old plastic potty chair in the middle of the living room.

"Where did you get that?" I asked, noticing the scratches and specs of dirt. Gosh, I hoped that was dirt.

"You know ol' Duane?" I didn't. "Well, his wife used to bring this with her when she went to the square dance hall. The lines for the bathroom at that place were atrocious!" Was she saying this was used by an *adult*? I didn't have time to process the question before she continued. "Jennifer, you go out and have a good time! I got everything under control here."

"Thanks so much, Yaya," I said. "I hope you know how much I appreciate it."

"I'm just happy to do it, Jennifer. Lord knows I don't want

anyone's life to be as hard as mine was!" She laughed in a weary yet bemused way, as if remembering a heartbreaking movie that ultimately had a happy ending. Yaya had a difficult childhood in a family so poor that bits of cornbread were sometimes the dinner entrée. For years they had no electricity, and when she went to high school her family still had no running water. When Joe was four years old, she ended up a single mother after an unwanted divorce. With only a high school education that was interrupted by farm work, she struggled to provide for herself and her son. She was often unable even to run the heat or the air conditioning because she couldn't afford it.

I thanked her again and escaped to the car with the kind of uneasy desperation of a burglar who'd just triggered the security alarm. As an introverted child raised by quiet, cerebral parents, my life up until this point had been one with a whole lot of silence. Decades of living in big houses with few people had carved deep grooves into my habits; I had a great need for quiet and for complete control of my surroundings. Sometimes it felt like my current life was a macabre psychological experiment to see exactly where the mental breaking point was for someone with my temperament.

Yaya was only here for a short visit, so I had to make the most of this opportunity to enjoy myself. My mom lived nearby and often helped Joe and me sneak out for date nights, but she had a full-time job so I almost never had help with the kids during the day. Today, I knew exactly what I would do: I'd visit my favorite bookstore.

Every time I came here, when I first walked in the door, I acted like the guy in the escape scene in *The Shawshank Redemption*. My experience of the world had become so limited that it was a glorious sensory feast to enter the place. Everything from the colors of the covers to the screech of the espresso machine in the coffee shop felt new and exciting. My body actually tingled at the knowledge that each book was packed with ideas and stories; I felt swept up in the electric current of human inspiration just standing near them.

A small, round table in the corner of the cafe was empty as if it had been waiting for me. It was just big enough to hold my enormous black laptop, for which, I now realized, I had forgotten the charger cord. I opened the screen to see that I had an hour of battery left. I pulled up the page for my blog and typed in the title for my latest update.

I had started this blog when Donnell was a baby and I was exploring the topic of spirituality. As someone with no faith background before I had my own religious conversion, this was an outlet for my many thoughts and questions on the subject. I used to update it only a couple of times per month, but recently I'd been enjoying it so much that I was starting to take it more seriously.

The words flowed with the same pent-up power as water exploding through floodgates in a dam. I'd left the house bedraggled and tense; now I sat up straight, my expression bright and alert. As the essay took shape, I relished the process of taking a jumble of thoughts and turning them into something comprehensible. Just as some women get a great rush of peace after tidying their houses, I experienced the same kind of rush when I tidied my thoughts. It was as if my mind had been a disaster area on par with our living room at the end of the day, and now I was finally getting a chance to put everything in place.

When the update was finished, I leaned back and enjoyed the orderliness of it all. With seven minutes of battery remaining, I hit publish. I closed my laptop and rested my elbows on the lid, lost in the bliss of the moment.

When I did this kind of work, it was as if some dormant part of me came alive. It was more than just a hobby; it felt like a way of connecting with the world—the way I was *meant* to connect with the world. It was my theory that everyone has some kind of skill or hobby like this, like my programmer friend who had a side business making scented candles, or my grandfather, an engineer who became a self-taught gourmet chef in retirement. Joe's friend Keith called this a "blue flame," the passion that ignites a fire within you when you do it. Writing, storytelling—this was my blue flame.

My thoughts were interrupted by a burst of high-pitched greetings from a nearby table. A woman who'd been sitting alone recognized someone she knew, and now they were exchanging hellos in friendly southern accents. The woman who'd just arrived had a daughter with her who looked to be about two years old, the same age as Donnell.

"She's getting so big!" the seated woman remarked, setting aside her book to gaze at the girl, who instinctively inched closer to her mother.

I was about to drift back into my daydreams when the standing woman said, "My sitter's with the baby, and when she comes I like to have a little one-on-one time with Mackenzie." She ruffled her daughter's hair. Her daughter looked up at her mother with a smile of pure contentment.

The high I'd been riding after finishing the blog post evaporated. My bliss was gone, now replaced with a heavy pall of guilt.

"I'm home with them all day," Mackenzie's mom continued, scooping up her daughter as she spoke. "But when I can get a little free time—which I hardly ever do!—I think it's so important to have this kind of quality time, you know?"

The other woman, who seemed to be about a decade older than her friend, nodded approvingly.

"Good for you. You'll have plenty of free time when the kids are older. You need to treasure these moments with your little ones while you have them."

I half expected a film crew to pop out from behind the shelf of atlases and announce that this was all part of a hidden-camera show where failing parents were confronted. A man would introduce himself to me as the producer of *Bad Mom Intervention*. With cameras hovering in my face, he'd explain that his writers had spent days crafting lines for this actress to deliver that would perfectly contrast her with me to reveal all of my failings at once. "They did an amazing job," I would reply dryly.

But no such camera crew appeared, and, evidently, this saint-mom was describing her real life. It reminded me of a moment at one of the last playdates I attended. We moms were sitting on the floor in the hostess' playroom, taking turns talking about what we did with our time on the rare occasions that we had childcare help. I had my answer ready: "I run screaming from my house as fast as I can, and I have a margarita if it's an evening babysitter! Who's with me?" I pictured my statement being met with an uproarious round of high-fives. Luckily, other women answered first. One mom said quietly that she enjoyed spending extra time doing alphabet flash cards with her three-year-old. Another said she used sitter time to clean and decorate her home, sometimes adding a vase of fresh flowers for a touch of beauty. When my turn came around, I mumbled some lie about cleaning and cooking.

Whenever I had free time, I always appeared to be running away from my family. Really, it wasn't as much that I was running *away* from them as it was that I was running *toward* my blue flame. But seeing myself in contrast with this woman who spent her babysitter day with her daughter was a wake-up call. At that same playdate where I almost outed myself as the Margarita Maniac Mom, one of the other ladies admitted that she was exhausted and never had time for her own interests anymore.

"Our little ones need us right now," she said. "But before we know it they'll be grown and off to school. It's not too much to ask to give of ourselves for this short season in our lives." Someone else in the room actually whispered, "Amen."

I looked at the blog post I'd just written. In the document next to it was a list of other essays I planned to write this week, which would probably all involve letting the kids sit in front of the TV for hours. I needed to stop taking this so seriously. I could dash out a few updates here and there, but this was not the right season of life to dive into my personal passions. I had more important responsibilities right now. And, as the woman at the playdate pointed out, these years would pass quickly.

I reached for the keyboard to make one last edit on the post. Just as I started typing, the battery died, and the screen flickered to black.

3

At Least We Have Queso

JOE WAS CHOPPING GREEN BELL PEPPERS when he looked up and said, "We need to talk."

I checked to make sure the kids were still playing happily on the back porch and pulled out a chair to sit down at the kitchen table. I noted that no one has ever followed that statement with good news. It was never, "We need to talk: The International Astronomical Union is naming a galaxy after me," or, "We need to talk: A mysterious benefactor just gifted me a Lamborghini."

"Our account is overdrawn again," he said. "This morning I made the final payment to the mechanic for the transmission work, which took another big chunk out of savings." As he spoke he turned from the center island to the stove to dump the chopped peppers into a bubbling pot of melted cheese.

"Speaking of cars . . ." I said.

"Yeah. I know." Both of our cars were four-door sedans, which we thought would be fine for a soon-to-be family of five. What we had only recently realized is that you can't fit three car seats in the back seat of a mid-sized vehicle. "I found used minivans on Craigslist. If we get a basic model that's four or five years old we can get a good price, but even with what we've saved up we're still a thousand dollars short."

I hunched over the table and put my head in my hands. "Any ideas?"

"I guess I could ask George for a raise at some point," Joe continued, referring to his boss at the small law firm where he worked. "But I'd have to put in a bunch of extra hours for that to make sense."

Joe diced a white onion, which would soon be added to the pot on the stove. I couldn't help but smile as I watched him work, since he was bringing his usual type-A intensity to this queso. When he found our grocery store options for Mexican cheese dip lacking, he didn't just look up a better recipe. He researched the history of queso as well as the history of all of the ingredients of queso. (The day he did this, I knew exactly what he was up to because every few minutes I'd receive new emails from him with subjects like *Queso blanco vs. queso flameado—important differences.*)

It was this side of his personality that made his current work situation one of the most surprising turns of events in our lives. Joe grew up poor, in a neighborhood where few kids went to college and some ended up in prison. But Yaya was determined to break the generations-long cycle of poverty in her family. With that special ability to ignore every obstacle in her path that made her like a human hurricane, Yaya insisted that Joe go to college at Harvard or Yale. She was utterly unconcerned about the facts that no one in her family had ever gone to college, she didn't know where these schools were located, she knew nothing about the admissions process, and she wasn't even sure what an "SAT test" was. Joe set his sights on Yale, choosing that school because his favorite cartoon character, Snoopy, often flew a blue Yale flag on his doghouse as an homage to the cartoonist's alma mater.

After working feverishly in high school to achieve this dream, Joe went to Yale on financial aid and graduated in three years with honors. From there he went to Columbia Law School. After working at big-name law firms in New York, he wanted to move into the business side of things, so he went to Stanford's Graduate School of Business, and, while at Stanford, took masters-level coursework in computer science with a specialty in artificial intelligence. (This was such a departure from his family culture that when Yaya drove with him out to Stanford, she kept asking him if this "Stancliff" place was a reputable institution.)

When I met Joe, he had just moved to Austin for an executive role at the tech company where I was settling in to my first real job. I was twenty-three, just out of undergrad at the University of Texas; he was thirty, just out of business school. Joe carried with him every bit of the breathless desire to achieve that you'd expect from someone with his background, and I was more than happy to join him. When we got married we lived in a twenty-first-floor loft in downtown Austin. We traveled the country and the world, sometimes getting upgraded to First Class thanks to Joe's mileage status. Both of us regularly worked twelve-hour days. We often met for dinner after 10:00 p.m. because neither of us could get out of the office before then.

The life we crafted for ourselves back then was very entertaining and very shallow. We yearned for deeper connections with our friends but found them oddly hard to form when everyone was tipsy and shouting over techno music at a packed bar. All of our loved ones lived alone: Yaya had been single for decades, my parents divorced around the time I got married, and my grandfather was my last living grandparent. Joe and I were both only children, and my dad was also an only child, which made me my grandfather's only grandchild. When we saw them at holidays, we said we'd visit more often, but everyone knew we wouldn't.

That yearning for something deeper, something more, only intensified after we found out we were expecting Donnell, and it thrust us both into what could only be described as a spiritual awakening. Joe started out as a nonpracticing Christian who no longer read the Bible and never went to church; I was a lifelong atheist who once equated belief in God to belief in the Tooth Fairy. We thought we were simply asking theoretical questions about the existence of the divine. We imagined our quest would involve some meaty reading and perhaps a couple of quiet prayers in a scenic holy place. What happened instead was that God burst into our lives with all the subtlety of a neutron bomb, shattered everything we thought we knew, snatched our carefully crafted life plans and set them on fire, then gave us a big hug and tossed us onto a path we could have never imagined for ourselves.

We felt profoundly "convicted," to use our new religious parlance, to reset our priorities. Joe had grown up without a father in his day-to-day life, and he realized that if he stayed on the career track he'd been on, he wouldn't be much of a presence in his own children's lives. He left behind almost everything he'd worked to build in the first decade of adulthood and set off in a new direction.

And this lifestyle overhaul came at a cost: the calculation Joe had made when he'd gotten those expensive graduate degrees was that he would eventually earn a substantial salary. Now, his income was less than half of what it used to be, and our monthly student loan payments were enormous. We had discussed me going back to work in the tech world, but it didn't make sense for a few reasons. My skills were out of date, and I doubted that I currently had the mental capacity to navigate highly technical interviews, considering that this morning it had taken me three tries to come up with the word *potato*. Also, childcare costs for three children under age three would eat up most of the salary I could expect to earn.

Until this point, we were happy with these choices. We'd moved from downtown to the outskirts of the suburbs and bought an inexpensive three-bedroom home. His new job at a small, family-owned law firm involved pleasant work and a friendly environment. He'd been working there almost a year now, and he had never once brought stress home from the office. When we spent time together in the evenings, he was fully present to both me and the kids. In fact, it seemed like he had finally become the person he was meant to be now that he wasn't pouring every last drop of his energy into his career.

Yet now I was starting to question it all. This job, as pleasant as it was, barely paid the bills, and I worried about the pressure that that put on him. On top of that, now that I was in the third trimester, he often cleaned the kitchen, gave both kids baths, put them in pajamas and got them to sleep—all after a long day of work.

"I feel like you're going to collapse if you push yourself any harder," I said.

When Joe looked up from the cutting board, his eyes burned with tears. "I agree. I'm starting to feel really maxed out. But what choice do we have?"

I was shocked to see him so upset. "Oh my gosh. Are you crying?"

He chuckled and wiped his face with a napkin. "No. I just learned the hard way not to rub your eyes after you've been chopping jalapeños."

I was relieved, but there was no question that he was shouldering an enormous burden. We both fell silent for a moment, lost in thought.

Finally, he said, "At least we have queso."

Family Planning (and Other Things I'm Not Good At)

I SAT NERVOUSLY IN MY OBSTETRICIAN'S OFFICE. I wasn't nervous about the checkup but about the fact that I'd had to bring Donnell and Lane with me. So far they were both content to sit in the double stroller, but I sensed that the calm was tenuous.

"Okay, it's almost the big day!" the nurse said. "How are the shots going?"

I lifted my shirt just enough to reveal my stomach, which was covered in splotchy bruises and tiny, red dots where needles had pierced my flesh. During my second pregnancy, I had developed a deep vein thrombosis, a dangerous blood clot in a major vein. It turned out to be caused by a rare, genetic blood clotting disorder that I had inexplicably inherited from both parents (I immediately assured my hematologist that, as far as I knew, my parents did not meet at a family reunion). Now, whenever I was pregnant, I had to give myself blood thinning shots in the stomach every day.

She winced. "Well, you're almost done. Any names picked out?"

Joe and I originally thought we would name our kids after family surnames, Donnell representing our Scottish heritage (pronounced like the MacDonnell name), and Lane named for some Texas kinfolk. Our conversions inspired us to switch to saints' names, so this new baby would be Lucy Margaret Mary. As I explained this, the nurse half-listened. Her mind seemed to be on what she had to bring up next.

"So, there's one other thing," she said. "Look, I'm not trying to be a nag. I just wouldn't feel comfortable if I didn't bring this up again."

"Contraception?"

"Yes, contraception. I know you say you're sticking with the Natural Family Planning thing. Tell me about that decision, Jennifer."

"How much time do you have?" I joked.

Natural Family Planning is a method of child spacing where a woman determines the few days a month that she's fertile and watches a lot of TV with her husband during that time if they're not ready for a baby. NFP is often confused with the ineffective "rhythm method" and is stereotyped as being an utterly useless method of birth control—and Joe and I were doing a lot to further that stereotype. But we were aware that it could, theoretically, be effective, and we were committed to sticking with it.

Part of the decision was practical: because of my disorder, I could not take any hormonal contraception due to the increased risk of blood clotting. I was too indecisive to go the route of permanent sterilization, and the various other contraceptive options were either too ineffective or unappealing for other reasons that I was really hoping I wouldn't have to detail for this nurse.

But the other part of the decision was made on an entirely different level. The spiritual journey that Joe and I took ended up with us both becoming Catholic, which is the last belief system either of us ever imagined we'd belong to. If the nurse had time for me to explain it all, she would see how animated I became when I described how my newfound theology influenced this decision. I could tell her all about how I came to agree with the old-school Catholic view that abstinence-based methods of child spacing are preferable to contraception. (I'd probably stand up and pace wildly when I related it all to Aquinas' description of Natural Law, since that part was just so exciting.) But life experience had taught me that if one were to make a list of Top Casual Conversation Subjects That Nobody Cares About at All, "Your stance on contraception vis-à-vis your religious beliefs" would make it into the top three, right next to "The weird dream you had last night" and "Whether that rash is an allergic reaction or a fungal infection."

I spared the nurse the details and just said, "I'm Catholic. I don't do contraception."

"My sister-in-law is Catholic. I don't think a lot of people pay attention to that rule anymore."

I shrugged. "I know. But it's what works for me."

"So you want to have baby after baby?"

"No. No, we're done for a long time after this one. We've got it under control with Natural Family Planning." She looked pointedly at my protruding stomach. "We're working on it."

The nurse sighed. "Do you understand how much, umm, *sacrifice* is involved when you're first learning NFP?"

I said I did. And I didn't exactly look forward to that. But in the short time that I'd been using this system of family planning, it had changed almost every aspect of my life. I had discovered that it was more of an alternative lifestyle than just another way to avoid pregnancy. It strengthened my marriage, made me rely on my faith more than I ever would have otherwise, and it had given me another gift as well, one that I never expected to receive.

All my life, I had been uncomfortable with my body; in fact, it was a discomfort that bordered on hatred. It started in childhood, when my unusually tall height and unruly hair made me the target of endless teasing, and, eventually, bullying. In my teens and early twenties I dieted and exercised and obsessed about my appearance so that I could look how women were evidently supposed to look.

Meanwhile, I had a vague revulsion for all of those odd female things my body did, to the extent that I thought about them at all. In eighth grade health class we were taught about female cycles and fertility in conjunction with a teen pregnancy prevention program, and so it was all discussed with the same shroud of fear and suspicion as one might speak of witchcraft. I remembered the teacher showing us a graphic video of childbirth. When it was over, she switched on the lights and announced to our stunned and queasy class, "That's what will happen to you if you're not careful!"

That class comprised 90 percent of my education about the inner workings of the female body in my younger years.

The result of all of this was that I felt at war with my body. I resented my stomach's cravings for food when I was always trying to lose a few more pounds to look like the women in the magazines. I was baffled by fluctuations in my monthly cycle. I knew little about pregnancy or childbirth. In college, I once heard someone say that a woman's fertility fluctuates with her cycle, and she's only fertile a couple of days out of each month, but I didn't think that could be right.

I tried to assure myself that I was a strong, empowered woman. I would have never admitted this to anyone, but the naked truth was this: I was uncomfortable with almost every aspect of the female body.

Motherhood and my newfound faith had helped to heal some of this discomfort, but when I started learning Natural Family Planning, everything changed. In order to be good at this system of child spacing, you have to develop an intimate knowledge of how your body works. I was amazed when I learned about the intricacies of the female reproductive system. I'd stay up late, poring over books with purple or pink binding that featured pictures of flowers on the covers (for some reason they all looked like this), sitting up in bed and whispering aloud, "Why didn't anyone ever tell me this?"

I started to appreciate the differences between men's and women's physiology. I learned what optimal health for a woman really looks like, which led me to a natural revulsion toward the starving-skinny look I once forced myself to adopt. When I actually started getting to know my body, I finally stopped fearing my body. And when I stopped secretly loathing all of those perplexing things my body did, I stopped secretly loathing myself.

What I wanted to say to this well-meaning nurse was this:

"Yes, I do have some concerns about sticking with NFP, but it has given me something that years of introspection and self-help books never could. This practice has given me a sense of inner freedom I never thought I could experience. So, yes, I do have questions about what my future will look like with this type of birth control. But I also have no doubt that I am doing exactly what I need to be doing right now." Instead, I fidgeted self-consciously.

"It sounds like I'm not going to get you to take this?" She held up a brochure from a pharmaceutical company about a new device that sterilized women more permanently than their competitors. The model on the cover was very thin and very tan and held her arms in the air to symbolize her freedom.

"No thanks," I said.

The nurse held my gaze for a second. A concerned look flashed across her face before she replaced the brochure on the rack. The quick look she had given me seemed to say, "Are you sure you understand what you're getting yourself into?"

If the day had ended there, it would have been a great Girl Power moment for me. I stood up for my counter-cultural principles, reaffirmed myself in my own beliefs, and now I could maneuver the unwieldy double stroller off into the sunset.

Unfortunately, that's not how the doctor's visit ended.

Just as we finished the appointment, Donnell and Lane began crying. They had now been out long enough that they were morphing into Red Zone Children, incomprehensible beings who have no sense of logic or reason and have only two missions: destroy and make noise. And like Bruce Banner morphing into the Incredible Hulk, Red Zone Children also have superhuman strength and ability that mere mortals cannot overcome. I hadn't even made it out to the waiting room when Lane tried to escape her seat.

I picked her up, put her on my hip, and pushed the behemoth stroller with one hand. When I got to the exit that led into the waiting room, I had to hold the door open with my back while I pulled the front of the stroller through, carrying a very wiggly Lane all the while.

Next, Donnell jumped out. I set Lane down to chase after him, and she crawled back into the exam area. I scooped her up, then tripped over a wheel as I went to find Donnell. The kids were shouting, and I was so exhausted and over it that I began shouting too, which startled the people in the waiting room. It occurred to me how this must look, an enormously pregnant woman waddle-running after one toddler while carrying another. I considered shouting over my shoulder, "Hey guys, I do NFP! Want to join me?"

By the time I got everyone into the car, I was too tired to drive. I closed my eyes as I sunk back into the seat, imagining how much easier this trip could have been if I'd just brought a lasso.

The kids were both quiet now, and I could actually think for the first time all day. And in that silence, a thought elbowed its way into the forefront of my mind. It was a disconcerting idea that haunted the periphery of my consciousness, but one that I usually managed to shut down before it got through:

I might not be done having babies.

The idea brought its crazy friends too, namely, *I might not even want to be done having babies* and *We might have another kid sooner than I think.*

Around the time we found out we were expecting Lane, Joe and I realized that something felt right about having a big family—four, even five kids. Part of it was pragmatic: since our children would have neither cousins nor aunts nor uncles, they would have no extended family after Joe and I were gone. All they would have is one another. But, mostly, the decision was spiritual. Through my fledgling efforts at prayer, I had determined early on in my conversion that Joe and I were meant to be open to children on a level that most people would think is nuts.

Logically, nothing made sense about this. Every day was a new reminder that I lacked all the necessary skills one needs to be a competent housekeeper, and worries that I was failing my children were ever-present. I hadn't even seen a big family in action in my entire life. My mom was one of six children, but we always lived thousands of miles away from those aunts and uncles, and none of them went on to have big families themselves (I had only five cousins on that side of the family). Despite all of this, I once believed that there was something good unfolding here, and that I would find it if I stayed open to this calling.

But now all of that confidence was gone. Yes, I felt some nudge from the divine to have lots of kids. There was even some part of me, buried so deep in my subconscious that it resided next to secrets like my opinion that the Backstreet Boys' *Millennium* album was a masterpiece, that thought that having more babies sounded good. But it simply did not seem like something we could actually do.

Ever since the moment at the bookstore coffee shop, I'd been fantasizing about what my life could be like five years from now, when all my kids were at school. I pictured myself strolling back from the bus stop and entering my beautiful home (not the overcrowded house with the scary carpet we currently lived in—in this fantasy I was living in last week's Pottery Barn catalogue). I'd pour myself a cup of coffee, the sloshing of the steamy liquid the only sound in the house. I'd be surrounded by silence and order. Best of all, I would write guilt-free since the kids were at school.

Maybe I would reconsider this idea to have a big family one day. After these three kids were well into their school years, perhaps we could be open to another baby. But not now. If nothing else, I was pretty sure I would go crazy if I saw another positive pregnancy test and therefore had to hit the reset button on getting my own life back.

Beer Bong Playdate

THE KNOCK ON THE DOOR WAS THE WORST SOUND IN THE WORLD.
Soggy corn flakes floated in puddles of milk on the table and the
entry hall looked like a children's shoe factory had exploded in it. I
hadn't put on makeup or brushed my hair.

"Our friends are here!" I said, using the same tone I might use
to announce that the repo man was here.

I hated myself for scheduling this playdate. This woman, Hallie,
had found me through my blog. I'd posted a few pictures of our
church that made her realize we lived in the same area, and she'd
gotten in touch to suggest that we get together. I'd ignored her email
for weeks, until one afternoon I spontaneously dashed out a reply to
invite her over.

My life had changed so dramatically, so quickly, that my social
network had been demolished. Just a few years before, I lived in a
different part of the city with a different lifestyle and a different
belief system. I still liked my old group of friends in downtown
Austin, but our paths hardly ever crossed these days. When we did
get together, our conversations were stilted because our lives were
on such different trajectories now. Up here in the suburbs, I'd been
so overwhelmed just managing my day-to-day life that I hadn't met
many people. When I found myself talking back to the hosts on
daytime television, I knew I needed some real-life friends. So I'd
invited this Hallie person over.

It felt a little risky to hand out my home address to a random
person from the internet, so I took the precaution of Googling her.
I intended to verify her claim that her husband worked at a nearby

church, but all I had to go on was their last name. Which was Lord. Alas, my search for *Lord* and *church* did not help me stalk this woman's family. As I made my way to the door, I could already hear the dramatic reenactment of this moment on one of those true crime shows Yaya watched. A narrator with a gravelly voice would say over foreboding music, "Jennifer Fulwiler walked to her front door, thinking that she was going to meet another mom. Little did she know that The Internet Killer was waiting on the other side . . ."

I opened the door to see a dark-haired woman who was either not an internet killer or very good at hiding it. She wore a black knit dress accented by a peach cardigan, and she held a plate of homemade cookies covered in plastic wrap in one hand. A baby girl sat on her hip, secured by her other hand. "We brought treats!" a little voice said. I looked down to see two boys, whose ages I estimated to be three and two, standing next to her.

"I'm sorry about the state of the house," I said as I led them into the living room, kicking toys out of my way as I walked. "I just can't deal with anything at the end of pregnancy," I explained. I let the implication stand that the house wouldn't look exactly like this if I weren't pregnant.

"It's fine; your home is lovely," Hallie replied. I appreciated the lie.

When we reached the kitchen, it occurred to me that I'd forgotten to go to the store—I had almost nothing to offer them to eat, even though it was lunch time. The kids escaped to the back porch while I rummaged through the kitchen to find something that would pass for a meal.

"Would you like some water or coffee, Hallie?" I asked, pretty sure that I had just mispronounced her name. "Is it *HAY-lee* or *HAL-lee?*"

"*HAL-lee.*"

The name elicited a surprise spark of joy in my mind. I'd had a beloved childhood pet named Halley, pronounced the same way. Lost in a flash of memories, it didn't occur to me that I shouldn't say what I said next: "Oh, I had a cat named Halley! He was great."

So I'd invited my guest to a trashed house with no food and promptly informed her that I'd given a male cat the same name that her parents had given her. This would teach her to contact strangers on the internet.

"Is it okay if they play with that?" Hallie asked, peering through the kitchen window to the back porch.

I followed her gaze. "I guess . . . wait . . . what *is* that?"

We both stepped outside to get a better look at the object that our five children had discovered in the sandbox. Joe had recently cleared out a few old boxes from the attic, and the kids had co-opted some of the junk as playthings.

"It's a bird feeder!" her son announced. With Donnell's help, he was pouring sand into a long tube through a funnel at the top.

"Honey, I don't think that's a bird feeder . . ." Hallie said.

Now I recognized it. "Is that? . . . It's a beer bong!"

"Mommy, what's a beer bong?"

"Nothing," Hallie and I said simultaneously.

Joe had mentioned that one of those boxes contained a few items from his fraternity days, and evidently our children were now holding the precious Sigma Chi beer bong. I looked at Hallie to figure out whether she was about to start screaming or just quietly take her kids and leave. I was pretty sure this was not the kind of thing that happened in her house, with her church-employee husband and her proclivity for whipping together baked goods. To my surprise, her face registered no revulsion.

"It's a sand toy, honey. It's fine," Hallie said to the kids, which I took as an opportunity to change the subject and invite her back inside.

We sat on the couch in the living room, me assuring her, as I did with all guests, that the stains on the fabric were dry and wouldn't get on her clothes. We made strained conversation about family life and the blogs we both read. When her kids had questions or needed something, she gave them her full attention and spoke to them in a soothing, motherly voice peppered with terms of endearment like "sweetie" and "honey." There was one hopeful moment of connection when it came out that we had similar faith backgrounds since she was also not raised in a Christian household. Just as we began discussing it, Donnell and Lane started fighting over a pair of steel scissors they'd managed to ferret out of some non-childproofed place in the house. By the time I returned to the conversation, the subject had fizzled.

The long minutes finally piled up into a respectable amount of time for a playdate. After a late lunch of cheese sticks that were four days past their expiration, black beans leftover from the night before, and the cookies Hallie had brought, enough time had passed that we could put this attempt at me playing hostess out of its misery.

She gathered her smiling, well-mannered children and ushered them out the door as Donnell and Lane engaged in what seemed to be a body slamming competition on the couch. After I broke that up, I ushered the kids down for naps, then returned to the living room to sink into my chair.

6

Viral

THE LIVING ROOM MATERIALIZED BEFORE ME, everything blurry, as I found myself in the trance-like state of waking from unexpected sleep. I twisted around to check the clock on the stove. I'd been asleep almost two hours since the playdate with Hallie. Amazingly, both kids were still napping.

Out of habit, I grabbed my laptop from the end table next to me. I opened the lid and typed in my password as I let out a long, decadent yawn. My email screen was still up from when I'd checked it earlier. I was about to click away when I noticed a note from an old coworker whom I hadn't spoken to in years. Subject: *Congrats!* Below that note were the names of three other distant acquaintances. *LOL, Wow–you're bigtime!,* and *Great stuff* were the messages in their subjects.

The phone on the table next to me rang and caller ID revealed that it was Joe. I hadn't even said hello before he started talking.

"Remember that thing you wrote a long time ago about what people's coffee orders say about their personalities?"

This was not the way I expected this conversation to begin, but I did know what he was talking about. When Joe and I first started dating, before blogs had entered the online scene, I'd created a website where I shared humorous essays on various subjects. It had gotten a good amount of traction at the time and had made for a fun way to relax after my long days working in the tech world. I hadn't updated it in the years since I'd found out I was pregnant with Donnell, and the traffic was basically zero these days. I couldn't imagine why Joe was bringing it up now.

"Get this," he said. "A lawyer from the firm downstairs was just telling me about this hilarious thing he read online about people and their coffee orders. Turns out he was talking about your piece! Then a friend emailed me about it as well. Everyone is talking about it!"

We finished the conversation and I hung up the phone in a daze. I pulled up the email account associated with the old website, which I hadn't looked at in forever. The bottom of the list of emails was all spam, but yesterday morning real notes started flooding in from people who saw the coffee piece. Not all of the messages were positive, but I didn't mind—my writing was getting traction again!

I spent the rest of the afternoon reading one email after another, then searching around to see all the blogs and websites that were talking about what I'd created. When the kids woke up I let them watch TV so I could keep reading. An electric energy surged through me as I absorbed the feedback on my work. It was thrilling to be back in the mix of things again, even for this fleeting moment.

The work that I did in my daily life was hidden. Nobody saw it but Joe and the kids, or maybe my mom if she came over for dinner. I missed being part of the marketplace of ideas and missed it desperately. That familiar ache came over me: the ache to ignite my blue flame, to do this work that I loved and share it with the world.

I wanted to ride the wave of momentum from this viral essay. I could offer to write freelance pieces for all the sites that were talking about this coffee piece. I could update my blog more often. At some point I could even think about writing a book, something I'd wanted to do since I was a child. And maybe all of this would translate into a little income, which would relieve the financial pressure Joe was under.

No sooner had these thoughts crossed my mind than I was brought back to the reality of my situation. It was the bookstore cafe incident all over again. *Not now*, I reminded myself. *Do what you need to do as a mom. Make the sacrifices. Get through it. This time will pass before you know it.*

Loaves of Bread

WITH DONNELL'S BIRTH, before my clotting disorder was diagnosed, I'd gone to a midwife-staffed birthing center. We had long conversations about how I could best be empowered in my birthing experience and carefully chose the scented candles that would burn in the room. Now that I had to have labor induced in a hospital to manage clotting issues, my birth strategy was so simple that I didn't even need to write it down. Plan for relaxation? *All the drugs you can legally give me.* Vision for how we handle the labor process? *I don't really have much of a say in the matter, do I? So let's go back to talking about the drugs . . .*

At the end of August, our new daughter, Lucy, was born. I had to stay in the hospital for three days, and I always enjoyed the time with just me and the new baby. When I changed her diaper for the first time after Joe and the rest of the family returned home, I stopped to gaze at this new person in front of me. My hospital bed was pushed up next to a picture window with a view of a courtyard, and the late afternoon light was so soft and perfect it looked like we were in a photo shoot for a greeting card. Lucy's little legs and arms moved erratically as her brain raced to figure out how all of this works, her chubby doll's face occasionally scrunching up in confusion. I closed my eyes, sitting in quiet gratitude for this gift I'd been given. It was never more clear to me than at moments like this that parenting was a sacred duty.

We'd only been home from the hospital for a week when the pressures of life made themselves present once again. I ended up delirious and feverish with what turned out to be mastitis. As soon as that was taken care of, Joe had to go back to work. On top of that, we still didn't have a car that fit the whole family.

Joe had his eye on a five-year-old minivan he'd found on Craigslist and was trying to figure out a way to get it. There was a time when I would have launched into a *Braveheart*-style rallying cry about how I could not be a minivan-driving person; now I would have happily driven the Oscar Meyer Wienermobile if it fit three car seats. Joe had been in touch with the owner of the minivan and was pretty sure it wasn't going anywhere, but we were still a thousand dollars short.

One evening we were sitting in the living room after the kids went to bed, me reading P.G. Wodehouse with the baby sleeping in my arms, Joe doing something on his laptop. The baby and I both jumped when he let out a startled shout.

"What is it?" I asked.

"This deposit into our checking account. Did you make that?"

"No. What deposit?"

"It's for eight hundred dollars!"

"No way. Let me see." He turned around the laptop. Sure enough, there was a deposit for $812.77.

"It wasn't a check," Joe said. "It was an electronic direct deposit, but I don't recognize the company name that sent it."

"Wait." I leaned in to get a good look at the organization's name. "I do." This was from the company that served ads on my old website where I wrote humor essays. "I completely forgot that I still had ads up on that coffee order piece that went viral again. This must be revenue from all the traffic it got."

Joe moved to take the laptop back but I grabbed it to stop him. I wanted to look at the number for another long moment, to savor this symbol that so many people had responded to something I created. The traffic on that page was now back to almost zero, but that dollar amount symbolized my brief return to the marketplace of ideas.

"Want to hear something crazy?" Joe said when I finally released the computer. "My mom just gave me a late birthday check for two hundred dollars. We now have exactly enough money to get the minivan."

"Oh, wow." There was a saying in Catholic circles that "every baby comes with a loaf of bread under its arms." Originally conveyed to me by a woman whose grandmother raised nine children in an abandoned boxcar in Mexico, the idea is that unexpected graces always come into your life when you're open to the people whom God sends your way, whether it's babies or friends in need or anyone else. I couldn't help but call that phrase to mind now, even though the skeptic in me had always hesitated to embrace it.

As if Joe heard my thoughts, he said, "They say that every baby comes with a loaf of bread under its arms!"

"Well, I don't think we can say that this ad revenue was dropped down from heaven or anything."

Joe looked at me with knowing amusement. "Old atheist habits die hard, huh?" Despite his doggedly linear way of thinking and his rigorous academic training, he was usually the one of the two of us who was most open to seeing the divine hand at work in our lives.

"I'm just saying that I doubt it's God's top priority to send me cash from some smack-talking thing I wrote when there are people all over the world who need this money a whole lot more than we do."

"Yeah. I'm not suggesting that God is a big ATM machine in the sky."

"Then what are you saying?"

"I don't know. Maybe it's not about the money per se. Maybe God is trying to get your attention."

Whether it was God or just a fortunate turn of events, it was quite effective at getting my attention. In the weeks that followed, I kept thinking about it. I had wanted to jump back into this work when this essay first went viral, but now that I saw that I could potentially bring in some income from it, my excitement had doubled in intensity.

I told myself over and over that I could get back to it soon enough, but I just had to wait until the kids were older.

You're doing the right thing. This is what good mothers do. It'll go by quickly.

I repeated these words like a mantra, as if I could force myself to believe that they were true if I just said them enough. The reality was that I had no peace. Now that Lucy was here, that sense that we were meant to have a big family had only grown stronger. The fact that more babies continued to feel right, even in the midst of the absolute chaos that came with having three children under age three, made me think that it definitely had to be some special call from God. And I was starting to see that I simply could not keep ignoring it.

So what, then, of my personal passions? If I did have more children, when would I ever get to this work that I loved?

I was trying to follow the roadmap to perfect motherhood, but I only felt more lost every day. I walked around in a state of perpetual unease and confusion, kind of like how you feel just before you realize you have the wrong map.

A Friendship Is Born

I CRADLED THE PHONE ON MY SHOULDER so that I could use both hands to stir baby food. I had called Hallie to offer her congratulations on her fourth pregnancy. She and I had gotten together a few more times since the infamous beer bong playdate the summer before, and now we talked by phone to trade recipes or swap parenting tips once or twice a month. I still had trouble connecting with someone who was so much better at life than I was, but I increasingly enjoyed her company. I was asking Hallie if she had any names picked out when Donnell and Lane turned up the TV in the living room to "cosmic blast" level.

"I'm sorry, Hallie," I shouted as I rushed for the volume button. "They always do this. There's this song about that old cartoon, *Jabberjaw*. The cartoon network plays it during the commercials about a hundred times a day, and the kids turn up the volume every time it comes on. They have this special dance they do . . ."

"Oh, that's so funny! That's—" I didn't hear the rest of what she said because of Donnell and Lane's protests that I'd ruined their dance.

"I'm sorry, what did you say?" I asked when I got them settled down.

"*Jabberjaw*—that's Dan's band's song!"

"Dan who?"

"Dan, my husband!"

"I don't think I follow . . ." She was clearly misunderstanding me. This song was by a punk band whose name I was vaguely familiar with from when they toured through Austin in the late nineties. I wasn't sure what the connection was to her church-employee husband.

"The song is by the band Pain, right? That's Dan. He was the lead singer. That's so funny—I could hear his voice in the background when the song came on."

I needed a minute to process this. I had listened to and commented on this song dozens of times before—just last week I'd joked to Joe that it was the soundtrack to my crazy life right now. It came on the television so often that I knew all the words. I might have even been to a Pain concert at some point in college. Hallie's husband was the lead singer?

"I'm so confused. I thought you said Dan works for a church," I said.

"That's his career now. The band was—" she stifled what seemed to be a wry laugh. "That was in his old life."

"So wait. How did you guys meet?"

"I went to see one of his shows when he played the Gilman in Berkeley. This probably sounds crazy but, as soon as he stepped out onto the stage, it was love at first sight."

This is not how I would have imagined that my devout homemaker friend met her husband. "Were you guys religious then?"

She laughed. "No. Not at all."

She went on to tell me the story of how, at age nineteen, she moved from her home in San Francisco to follow her new punk rocker boyfriend back to Mobile, Alabama—only to have him tell her shortly after she arrived that he had had a profound spiritual transformation and God might be calling him to be a monk. I shrieked and guffawed as she shared the details of this wild ride that led Dan to walk away from the band just as it was poised to become famous, and how all of this led to Hallie's own conversion to Christianity.

"As you can probably guess, Dan eventually decided that he wasn't meant to be a monk. And now we're about to have four kids!" Hallie said at the end of her story.

I shook my head in wonder at everything I'd just heard. "Okay, we need to talk."

"Sure. I think I have a few more minutes before the kids wake up from naps."

"No. I mean, get together in person, just the two of us, and *talk*." In the months of our burgeoning friendship, I had hesitated to open up to her. I imagined that she wouldn't be able to relate to someone like me, who didn't always fit perfectly into the mold of Happy Christian Mom. Now, after this conversation, the wall that had separated us had been demolished—or maybe I finally saw that it never existed at all.

We made plans for that evening, and when I got off the phone, I was jubilant. I gave seven-month-old Lucy a big mouthful of food, and we smiled at one another. A funny expression crossed her face, like she was happy but thinking about something, and I assumed it was her picking up on the joy in my demeanor.

"Things just might be looking up, right, Lucy?" I said to her.

She let out an explosive sneeze, and baby food splattered all over my face.

Joe was at the office late, but my mom kindly offered to babysit so that I could make this chat with Hallie happen. We met at my favorite bookstore, which was the first time I'd been back since the day I'd seen that mom spending quality time with her daughter. That memory inspired me to skip the small talk with Hallie. I spoke with the intensity of an investigative reporter about to crack the case of the century as I opened the discussion: "So you used to run in San Francisco cool-kid circles. You went to punk shows at the Gilman. Now you're a religious stay-at-home mom with lots of little kids. Was anything about that transition rough for you?"

Hallie seemed surprised but delighted by my bluntness, as if she'd been starved for real conversation, too.

"Are you kidding? Pretty much all of it. I've had to learn everything the hard way." Like me, she came from a small family—one sibling, in her case—and had little experience with kids and babies when she got married. Her mother was a strong feminist who ran a Neonatal Intensive Care Unit at a prestigious hospital in the Bay Area and had always hoped that her daughter would have an equally impressive career herself. "To be honest, I still struggle a lot."

"But you seem so perfect!"

She shook her head, her voice heavy with sincerity. "No, no. I'm far from perfect." She glanced over her shoulder as if to confirm that nobody else would hear us. Then she lowered her voice and said, "On Monday I went to the eye doctor's office, and it was one of those days, you know? The baby was up all night, the kids had colds, we had bills to pay. Anyway, I go in for my appointment, and they had rescheduled it without calling me, and now they couldn't get me in. They were completely unapologetic about it, even after I explained the insane amount of effort it took for me to get childcare to come out there. One woman actually rolled her eyes at me."

"Yikes. That's when I go sit in my car and cry."

"Maybe that's what I should have done."

"So what did you do?"

"I screamed at them."

"What?" I guffawed. "Seriously?" I could not imagine Hallie, with her impeccable manners and quiet, graceful demeanor, raising her voice at anyone.

"Yeah. It was bad. I was so loud that everyone else in the room stopped to stare." She leaned in closer, laughing as she spoke. "I feel like a crazy woman, Jen! I mean, I think they were probably about to call the cops! I seriously can never go back to that doctor's office again."

We giggled as I shared some of my own less-than-dignified

moments that had happened recently. I knew that it was probably not a compliment to my personality that I liked this woman a thousand times more now that I knew that she occasionally screamed at strangers, but I didn't care. It had been so long since I had had a real connection with someone who truly understood my life and shared my imperfections, I was overcome with wave after wave of relief.

We talked about everything: she told me that Dan had lost his job, and they were worried about him being able to find a new one. We discussed our shared concerns for the pressure that our husbands faced. I told her about my recently rekindled love of writing and the money I made from the old piece that went viral. I told her about how I thought I should set all of that stuff aside until the kids were older, and yet I had no peace about that decision.

"Yes!" she said, so loudly that the man next to us turned his head. "Oh my gosh, yes! I have been thinking about these exact same things! And, listen, we're not the only ones. I'm on an email list for the moms group at my church, and so many women are struggling with this stuff."

Thus began one of the most honest, fascinating conversations I'd had in years. Normally, I loved the ambiance of a bookstore coffee shop. I loved sneaking peeks at the stacks of titles people brought to their tables to peruse while they sipped their drinks. I was energized by the smells of the roasted beans and freshly bound books. But none of that existed to me now.

"Honestly, do you know any woman who has young children and is content with this area of her life?" I asked.

Hallie thought for a moment. "I mean, I'm sure they exist, but . . . no. No, I don't."

At Joe's office Easter party, the wife of one of his coworkers mentioned that she was starring in a play at the community theater. She had a one-year-old at home, and she couldn't even talk about her big role without mentioning the guilt she felt in every other sentence. Hallie had just gone to a women's group at church where a mom said that she used to be a musician in an orchestra.

"This sweet woman kept saying she was fine with setting aside her music to raise her kids, but she started tearing up before she could finish."

"Why don't we talk about this more often?" I said, my voice becoming more confident the longer this conversation went on. "Why do we have to whisper about these kinds of feelings like we're talking about having side jobs as drug dealers?"

Before Hallie could respond, I knew the answer to my own question—at least *my* answer. I rarely voiced these kinds of feelings to anyone except Joe because I was afraid that it would come across like I didn't love my kids. I worried that if I said "I am really unhappy with my life right now," it would come across like I was saying "I am really unhappy that I'm a mother." I didn't think anyone would understand.

Hallie and I talked for another hour about our mess of emotions on the subject, and then we both had to get home. We exchanged warm goodbyes and promised to chat tomorrow to continue the conversation. I walked to my car in the comfortable air of a late spring evening, my senses tuned to absorb every detail of this moment. Hallie and I didn't come up with any answers; we had no grand solutions to these problems that so many women like us faced. But I had something that was at least as good as a tidy solution and might even be better: the joy of encountering someone else who was asking the same questions.

Shot in the Dark

THAT NIGHT, AFTER EVERYONE ELSE WAS ASLEEP, I crept downstairs and grabbed my laptop. Cross-legged on the couch in my pajamas, I hunted among my files for a document that I hadn't looked at in years. I finally found it in an old folder, stored among a graveyard of unfinished essays, database schemas from old projects, and even a few college papers. I'd called it "*goals-writing.txt.*"

Even seeing the name sparked a warm happiness. I used to review this file almost weekly back when I was running the old website where I wrote the piece about people's coffee orders and their personality types. I clicked it open. When the words filled the screen, sensations of hope and excitement came with them, like a familiar smell on a favorite coat that had been stored away in a chest.

It was a list of everything I once dreamed of accomplishing. The bookstore conversation with Hallie had gotten me thinking: Was there some way I could get back to this work sooner rather than later? Was I missing something in my assessment of the entire situation? I had hoped that reviewing this file might spark some ideas.

Nothing grabbed my attention, and I was about to close the document. Then I noticed the very last note: *Pitch book idea to Ted.*

The two words *Ted* and *book* sent me careening back into a land of dreams that I hadn't visited in a very long time. Around the time Joe and I got engaged, a literary agent named Ted contacted me to introduce himself. He said that he'd come across my essays on my website and liked my writing style. He was starting a new literary agency and told me to let him know if I ever had a book idea I'd like to pitch to him. I was so thrilled at the prospect that I'd stayed up all night sketching out possibilities, but I couldn't pull a coherent vision together. Then wedding planning and marriage and babies got in the way, and now it had been years since we'd been in touch. With every month that passed, Ted grew more and more out of reach. He was no longer a new agent who might be open to taking a risk on unheard-of authors; sometimes I checked his agency website to keep up with what he represented, and I regularly saw bestselling titles.

Remembering all of this rekindled the strongest and most consistent desire of my life, like a flame blooming instantly when kindling is thrown onto glowing coals. For me, that was my desire to write a book.

It started when I was nine years old. At that time my dad had only recently recovered from colon cancer. Then, the economy crashed and he was laid off from his job as a construction project manager. Months went by, then a year, and he hadn't been able to find work. My mom's salary as a bookkeeper was spread dangerously thin, and the tension in the house rose daily. A family we knew had their home and most of their possessions taken away by creditors just a week before Christmas; another had a repossessed car towed away while the kids watched in their pajamas. At night I often heard my parents speaking in hushed tones in the kitchen, and I sometimes wondered if we were next. They did their best to shield me from the stress we were under, but worry was always present behind my dad's eyes.

But when we talked about writing books, his demeanor became light. He smiled easily as he explained a plot shift in his Special Forces novel, based on his experience as a Green Beret during the Vietnam era. He'd often let me stay up past bedtime because we were ensconced in front of the TRS-80 computer, hammering out the details of his book or mine. His enthusiasm was tireless as he helped me tighten the chapters in my novel, a thriller about a fourth grade girl's Machiavellian ascent up the social ladder of her elementary school. When we escaped into the land of stories, everything was okay again.

And sometimes we dared to dream of having our tales published. Books were woven into the fabric of our lives, spilling out from overstuffed shelves onto coffee tables and bedside stands. All three of us in our little family used the written word as our primary escape from the world, sometimes spending entire Sundays lounging in the den, each of us lost in a novel, the only sound the occasional turning of a page. In our many moves across the country, I often spent weeks, sometimes months, without a single friend—but books were always my escape hatch. For my dad and me, the idea of contributing to this world of the printed word felt like gaining admittance to a magical realm that we'd long admired but had only seen from the outside.

As I was pondering all of this, my hands drifted across the keyboard. I searched online for news about Ted's agency without even consciously deciding to do it. I scanned reviews for a few of the most recent books he'd represented. Then I typed his name absentmindedly into the search box on my email. I was only planning to look through my correspondence with Joe about Ted's agency, but the search suggested his email address.

I sat up straight, my body ready for action, though I had no idea what that action might be. Was this still a working address? He may very well have disabled this one and adopted a new one as his agency grew. I stared at it for at least ten minutes, trying to figure out what to do with this unexpected information.

I decided to shoot over a note—chances were that the email would bounce anyway. I typed up a quick message re-introducing myself. I let him know that I was planning to get back into the writing world one of these days. I also mentioned that I had a blog and that "multiple readers" had told me I should turn the subject matter into a book one day, which technically was true because Joe and Hallie had suggested it.

Before I could talk myself out of it, I sent it.

I waited for the immediate bounce-back of a disabled address. It didn't come.

I was realistic enough to know that I probably would not get a reply—literary agents are bombarded with dozens of legitimate queries per week and often don't have time to respond to all of those, let alone pointless notes from random people just saying hello. But this email wasn't about the reply. The message here was more to me than to this agent. It was a concrete act of hope, a signal to myself that I was not going to let go of my passions without a fight.

The next morning, I dashed out my first real blog update in more than a week, my words brimming with energy. I found out a few days later that Donnell and Lane were accepted into a Mother's Day Out program that our parish offered two mornings per week. On top of that, Lucy had started reliably sleeping through the night.

Just as we eased into this new season of routine and predictability, it occurred to me one morning that the timing of my cycle was off this month. I wasn't worried about it, but I grabbed an old pregnancy test from under the sink. I was in the middle of going through the motion of glancing at the result while tossing it into the trash when I froze. It was positive. Baby number four was on the way.

10

Wholeness of Vision

"WAS THIS PLANNED?" the nurse wanted to know when I came to the doctor's office to get my blood thinner prescription. It's hard to say whether she was more confused by the fact that I didn't have a clear answer to that question, or by the fact that I was already in there with another pregnancy in the first place.

The problem was that I didn't know how to answer. One of the salient features of Natural Family Planning is that the effectiveness level varies alongside your motivation level. If a woman were strongly motivated to make sure that pregnancy didn't happen in any given month, she could track her fertility signs meticulously and could likely get her NFP effectiveness rate up to around 98 percent. I'd just seen a study by the European Society for Human Reproduction and Embryology that showed that NFP, if practiced a certain way, was as effective as the birth control pill.

But in my case, NFP forced my secret feelings to the surface. It's a sacrifice-based method of birth control—and each month, when the time to make those sacrifices rolls around, it makes you question just how serious you are about avoiding pregnancy right now. As it turned out, Joe and I weren't that serious. The way I practiced it, my NFP effectiveness rate was probably about 70 percent.

"How do you not know if it was planned or not?" the nurse asked.

"Because I don't see the answer to that question as being binary but as residing on a spectrum," I said. I started to go into my spiel about how I no longer subscribed to the false dichotomy of "planned" versus "unplanned," but when she looked at me like I was insane I stopped.

After I picked up my first box of blood-thinner shots from the pharmacy, I started heading home. I was stopped at a light where I would turn left to go north to my house, but I surprised myself by jerking the steering wheel to go right instead—toward the church. Our parish held a noon Mass every weekday that lasted less than an hour. I pulled onto the highway going south, and soon the cross on top of the broad, bronze dome peeked out from behind industrial buildings up ahead.

I slid into a pew a few rows back from the front, the bag of shots from the pharmacy sitting next to me. The priest entered in a quiet processional, reciting the entrance antiphon as a poem since there was no choir at weekday services. On Sundays this grand building would be packed with a thousand people, but today it was only me and a hundred or so other attendees. The church had been constructed recently but had old-world character, its wide columns supporting a lofty, intricately designed ceiling with a long barrel vault that led to the ten-foot crucifix at the front of the sanctuary.

Everything about this structure radiated peace: the smooth lines of the architecture, the way the stained glass diffused the harsh summer sunlight into a warm glow. Behind the crucifix was an enormous replica of Raphael's painting *La Disputa*, in which philosophers' robes billowed gracefully under the rolling clouds of heaven. Even the air felt laden with the presence of God, thick with graces waiting to be bestowed. I closed my eyes, hoping that some of it would rub off on me.

I'd come here as an act of surrender. I'd been trying to run from that call to have a big family for years, and now it was time to give up. I had exhausted my ability to resist this plan for my life. It felt too right (and I was too incompetent with family planning) to keep fighting it.

And what I wanted in exchange for my surrender was peace.

I was happy about this baby, and even happy, in a way, about this strange plan for my life. But all of my concerns about managing my household and doing the work that I loved still filled me with worry.

I was kind of surprised when the Mass ended and I felt just as conflicted as when I'd arrived. I knew that I wasn't supposed to approach worship like I was bartering at a flea market, saying, "Hey, God, if I give you forty-five minutes of my afternoon, you have to give me peace and perfect clarity in return" . . . but that was kind of how I was hoping it would play out.

I was backing the car out of the parking place when I realized I'd forgotten my shots back on the pew, so I re-parked and rushed toward the church. The street value of that box was $2,000 (luckily my insurance paid for it), so I ran as if I'd left a diamond necklace inside. My pace slowed, however, when I remembered that the local black market probably didn't have big demand from people wanting to shoot blood thinner needles into their stomachs.

I retrieved the box and hurried back out, but when I pushed open the twelve-foot-tall oak door, I paused. A small crowd had gathered in front of the building, people kissing and greeting one another in the wide, paved courtyard. The church door closed with a hefty thud behind me, just as I sensed the message: *Stay. Watch.*

I felt powerfully drawn to wait and see what event was taking place, as if an unseen hand had gently grabbed my arm to stop me. There were about thirty people gathered, the ages ranging from elderly to newborn, and they all spoke Spanish. A young woman with a professional camera snapped pictures. I gathered from snippets of conversation that they were here for a wedding rehearsal.

Watching their warm greetings transported me back into some of my fondest childhood memories. My grandfather spent most of his adult life working as an engineer in Latin America, and my dad was raised in Mexico. Once my grandparents moved back to Texas, when they were in their sixties, they became tapped into the local community of recent immigrants. They used their fluency in Spanish to help folks navigate U.S. culture, and I had fond recollections of their living room being filled with loud, jovial conversation *en español*.

The Mexican community I knew then had an entirely different way of seeing the world, one in which more people meant more fun. As a kid, I noticed whenever we'd visit Tampico or Mexico City that our friends there seemed to live in this strange world where you didn't stress about new folks showing up, whether it was an unexpected pregnancy or a neighbor stopping by or a niece who needed to move in with her three kids for a while.

I appreciated this people-first lifestyle but never considered it to be something I would adopt for myself. My introverted, individualistic nature was at the very core of my identity. In fact, I'd already decided if this new baby were a girl, her middle name would be Frances, in honor of the fourteenth-century saint named Frances of Rome, who was so socially anxious that she collapsed from stress during the parties surrounding her wedding. That was me. I was the person who needed to minimize having people all up in my face. Inviting people into your life leads to unpredictability and noise and mess—all things I sought to avoid.

And yet this mentality had been eroding over the past few years. Now, I felt it start to crumble. People like this family here in front of me today seemed to understand something about the meaning of life that I would do well to understand myself.

The family gathered together for a group picture, presumably to commemorate this wedding rehearsal. They smiled in unison, and, just as the photographer began snapping rapid-fire pictures, a baby took off his mother's floppy sun hat and waved it in the air. The woman was attempting to get it back when a gust of wind whipped it out of her son's hands. Seconds later, the group would scatter as everyone scurried after the hat. But for a brief moment, the woman burst out in unexpected laughter, just as everyone turned toward her, their faces registering a mix of delight and confusion. The photographer got the shot.

It would be a fantastic picture: the hat floating above the baby, everyone's faces full of emotion. Certainly, it would make it into the wedding album. I could see this group of people gathering at a family party, perhaps a year from now, and chuckling together when they pointed to this shot. Then I imagined it being brought out decades later, perhaps at an anniversary celebration, and everyone would marvel at how young they looked in the picture. Then, one day, it would probably end up in a box in an attic somewhere. Perhaps, far in the future, someone would find it again. All the motion and vivid colors that I saw before me right now would be trapped behind a faded image. Many of the faces would belong to people who had passed on. The baby would now be an old man, and people would chuckle to see what he looked like as an infant.

Imagining the story arc of this family across the generations called a phrase to mind: *wholeness of vision*.

I'd first heard these words used by Sheldon Vanauken, author of the classic memoir *A Severe Mercy*. His late wife, Davy, had experienced a crisis pregnancy as a teenager and gave up the baby for adoption. Sheldon and Davy did not have children together, and after she died he went off in search of Davy's child, whom he called Little Lost Marion. When he found her, he encountered a delightful woman who worked as a nurse and had three children of her own. He grew so close to Marion that she thought of him as a father.

Vanauken wrote fondly of how Marion and her family enriched his life, as well as the lives of many others; clearly, the world was a better place with them in it. In his final years, this led him to reflect on the importance of having a "wholeness of vision" when it comes to new life. He could validate the difficulties that his beloved Davy faced with her unexpected pregnancy. But now, like reading a book to its finish, he could see that that situation, as painful as it was, was just one part of a much bigger story.

Wholeness of vision.

That is what I was missing in all of my tortured calculations about family size. That was, perhaps, the secret that our friends from Mexico understood that I was missing. When I thought of this pregnancy, or imagined others after it, my mind immediately conjured a picture of me fumbling for a diaper at three o'clock in the morning while cradling a screaming infant in one arm and shouting to Joe, "I CAN'T DO THIS!" I never imagined that same baby as a twenty-five-year-old passing the gravy at my Thanksgiving dinner table or as a fifty-year-old walking into my hospital room with a bouquet of flowers.

My controlling tendencies led me to fixate so much on my immediate problems that I couldn't see past them. I tended to live my life ruled by the tyranny of the immediate. I lacked a wholeness of vision, and I now saw that I'd never be able to accurately discern matters of family size without it.

I thought of our own funny pictures that had been snapped recently: Lucy sitting next to Joe, looking quite concerned as she monitored his work fixing a leak under the sink; Lane in her bright red pigtails, caught in mid-giggle as my dad read a book to her during one of his visits; Donnell holding a lamb when my mom took the kids to a petting zoo. One day these would be historic photographs, not casual depictions of recent events. They would represent people whose time on this earth had drawn to a close; their impact on the world fully known, their stories now complete. The daily problems I carried with me as I snapped each of these photos would be long forgotten. I needed to start making my big life choices with that perspective in mind.

The group now broke up, some people drifting into the church to start the wedding rehearsal. This moment had given me the peace I'd been searching for. I knew, when I looked at our family's life with a wholeness of vision, that the path of being unusually open to babies was the right one for us. I still had questions—a lot of questions, in fact—about what the details would look like. What about the fact that I was such a bad homemaker that the kids had goldfish crackers for lunch yesterday? What of my personal passions? Could I really be happy if my primary focus for years to come was managing a house full of babies? I walked back to my car with no answers, only a strong sense that, somehow, it would all work out.

11

For the Love of the Blob

WE PULLED UP TO MY GRANDFATHER'S HOUSE, now driving the minivan we'd been able to purchase thanks to the windfall after Lucy's birth. Yaya was already standing outside. She came to visit about once a month and had planned this trip to coincide with the birthday celebration we were doing for my grandfather. She had her cell phone cradled on her shoulder and appeared to be shouting into it as she approached the vehicle. When she slid open the side door to help us get the kids out, we could hear her end of the conversation. Indeed, she was shouting.

"I NEVER SAID I WAS GOING TO VOTE FOR THAT MAN! . . . that's not—no, that's not what I said . . . LISTEN, IF YOU WANT TO SUPPORT THAT SON OF A—"

"Good to see you!" I announced loudly to drown out the heated political argument, which was clearly going downhill. In between invectives, Yaya knelt down and hugged the kids, then stood to unstrap Lucy from her car seat.

She was now more interested in her grandchildren than in her phone call, so she offered succinct closing thoughts and hung up.

"Who were you talking to?" I asked as I took Lucy from her.

"Wrong number." She grabbed Donnell and Lane by the hands and turned to walk toward the front door before I had a chance to inquire further.

I followed Yaya down the walkway toward the house, a comforting sense of familiarity growing with each step. My parents and I moved across the country many times in my childhood, and so this house, my grandparents' home, was always a touchstone for me. I'd traveled this same path past the short, neatly trimmed bushes when arriving from our homes in Arizona, North Dakota, West Virginia, and Colorado, as well as countless times from our current home just one city over.

To step into the 1970s ranch-style home was to expect it to have the typical musty smell of an older house that had never been renovated, but the air here was always rich with scents of food—this time, the spicy aroma of ribs cooking on the back porch grill. Even though he'd just turned ninety-four, my grandfather, whom we called Papaw, regularly treated us to gourmet meals—in fact, he insisted on cooking this dinner, even though the celebration was for him. He delighted in pouring love into his only grandchild's family in the form of roasts and crepes and special desserts, all recipes he created himself.

My mom was already inside. Papaw was my dad's father, but my mom still made it to every dinner, even now that my parents were divorced. She often stopped by his house to have a lemonade with him after she played tennis or just to chat when she was running errands nearby. This was an enormous blessing, especially since my dad's job as an engineer still took him all over the place, his latest projects being in Abu Dhabi and the Cayman Islands. I pushed open the heavy sliding glass door to the back porch, where Papaw rested in between checking on the ribs. Yaya was already seated near the grill, and Lucy just about leapt from my arms to sit with her.

This porch with the simple concrete slab and rusting tin awning was the stage on which so many of my childhood memories played out: my grandmother feeding a squirrel from her hand when I was a young child; a great-uncle standing next to the grill in his cowboy hat, loudly telling a joke while Papaw dropped catfish fillets into a cast iron skillet full of bubbling oil; me holding a plastic cup of unsweetened iced tea, making polite chitchat with guests after my grandmother's funeral when I was fifteen.

I was soaking in the ambiance when Yaya said, "Jennifer, what are you writing these days?"

I'd just taken a seat in an old aluminum lawn chair with a cushion that was as dry and crumbly as month-old bread.

"I'm not really doing that anymore. Not right now, anyway," I said.

"Well, that's a shame. Last time we were here you were so excited when you talked about your blob."

"My blog?"

"Yeah, your blob or blog or whatever. You sure did seem to like that thing." She spoke of it as if it were a tangible object, which she may very well have imagined it to be.

"Yeah, it was fun to play around with. I still update it once in a while," I said. I forced myself to sound casual, but my tone sounded wooden instead, as if I were reading lines from a script. "My writing work is obviously not something I should be putting tons of effort into right now."

"I don't follow," Yaya said.

We paused as Papaw eased himself to a standing position, both of us watching in case he needed help. He slowly stepped over to the grill and opened the lid. A plume of white smoke mushroomed from inside, enclosing us in a fog that was infused with the rich scents of sage and rib meat.

"You know how it is: we've got a new baby on the way, I'm staying home with the kids. I guess I shouldn't be shirking my duties to mess around on the internet."

Yaya shot up in her chair and leaned forward in the determined posture she adopted when she was about to make a proclamation.

"Now wait a minute, Jennifer. Just wait one minute. You think you can't do your writing just because you're staying home with the children?"

"Well . . . sometimes, yeah."

"But it's something you like! How else are you going to take a load off with all these babies running around everywhere?" Right on cue, Lucy swung her chunky arm and knocked over Yaya's plastic mug, sending ice skidding across the ground. "Shoot, I'm worried about these kids if you *don't* work on this stuff you enjoy. You'll lose your mind!" she said with an astonished but jovial laugh.

I couldn't help but smile. Yaya was an endless source of wisdom, like if Yoda had an east Texas accent and a penchant for colorful language. Joe and I often referred to her as the Albert Einstein of common sense. She might need to call us four times to figure out how to turn on that VDF machine (DVD player), but her understanding of human nature and innate sense of what decisions will lead people to happy lives were second to none.

"I'm not even making money, you know," I said.

"Not yet, but if you keep at it you surely will. But that's beside the point." She turned in her chair to address my grandfather. "Papaw! Did your mother seem as stressed out as these young mothers today?"

Papaw set down the tongs on the platform next to the grill, which he'd built himself thanks to his expertise as a civil engineer. He closed the lid, and the air cleared. He slowly made his way back to the folding chair next to Yaya and eased himself into the seat.

"Oh, Lord, I don't envy these parents today. Everything is so . . . fast. Everyone is so busy."

"But your mother had such a hard life," I said. "I've heard your stories about how she'd hand-wash the laundry on a washboard with lye soap! My life is so much easier than hers was."

Papaw was born in 1914 and was therefore a living connection to a way of life that was about to be lost to history. He'd known plenty of folks who were born in the 1800s; he'd met men and women who lived through the Civil War. He was one of the last people to know the world before modern technology: his earliest memory was of attending a funeral where the coffin arrived in a horse-drawn hearse. He remembered life without phones or cars or even electricity. He was awed when he first saw a plane fly over-head when he was a teenager. And so I was interested to hear how Papaw would contrast my life to his mother's life.

"Oh, sure, Jenny, I don't think anybody's life was easy back then. We worked so hard in those days—'from can't-see to can't-see,' we used to say," he said, imitating the accent of his Texan loved ones by pronouncing *can't* so that it rhymed with *ain't*. He no longer had a southern accent after years spent working out of the United States, but he could bring it back effortlessly. "But life back then wasn't so stressful as it is today."

Yaya now leaned over to Papaw. "Did you know that parents can't even let their children out of their sight these days? What would your mother have done if she had to watch all the kids all day with everything else she had to do to keep the house and the farm going?"

Papaw laughed, "Oh, I don't know, but none of us would have liked it!"

"I used to send Joey out to play and just told him to come home when the street lights came on!"

"That's right," Papaw added. "My mama hardly saw us during the day. We'd roam around and hunt squirrels, go swimming in the creek when we weren't busy on the farm—usually barefoot, too."

My mom had stepped outside to bring Papaw a glass of water, and she chimed in.

"That was like us, too. When my brothers and sisters and I got home from school, we'd jump on our bikes and ride all over the neighborhood. Same thing during the summer. My mother had no idea where we were most of the time. Those were different times, weren't they?"

"And here's the other thing!" Yaya said, waving her index finger in the air to emphasize her point. "People back then weren't going, going, going all the time like you girls today. The way I lived, the way Papaw lived, you got some *rest* in the evening! Without TV or computers or all of these phones that blink and beep all the time, there just wasn't that much to do at night!"

Papaw nodded. "Once we had a radio, we would listen to that for a while, or maybe study for school by a kerosene lantern, but that was all we did after sundown. Then we'd go to bed—there wasn't much else to keep us up."

With smoke still lingering in the air like a hazy flashback scene in a movie, I imagined a typical evening in my grandfather's childhood farmhouse, everyone in that calm, subdued state that you fall into when you're in a room lit only by candlelight. I contrasted it to a typical evening in our house, all bright lights and half-pajama'd kids running down hallways to the soundtrack of endlessly dinging phones. I could picture Papaw's mother stepping out the front door of their hand-built wooden home in the afternoon, scanning the horizon for her kids, whom she hadn't seen since they bolted out the door after breakfast. She'd wipe her hands on her apron, ring the brass bell at the front of the porch, then put the last settings on the table before her husband and kids came in from the fields.

Since I'd become a parent, I'd had this idea that the perfect mother would spend hours out of each day on the floor with her young children, gazing into their eyes as she slowly articulated the sound of each letter on the educational wooden alphabet blocks they were building into a tower. She would take her four-month-old baby to Mom 'n' Me music classes and sit cross-legged on the floor, clapping her infant's hands to the beats of the nursery songs. Now I suddenly realized that mothers throughout history never did this; they never had time. Children's primary sources of entertainment were outdoor play and other kids, not their mothers.

Yaya took a moment to bounce Lucy on her lap, playfully nuzzling her face into the baby's chubby neck, then she returned to me.

"Here's what I'm saying, Jennifer: whenever you talk about all that writing stuff you like to do, you look *happy*. I think that your life as a young mom today is hard. It's not hard like Papaw's mom's life was—or, Lord, like my life was as a single mother—but it's hard in other ways. You never get to rest your mind. You're stuck in a house with the kids. You're supposed to have your eyes on them all day, every day. Everything's all a ruckus all the time, even at night. I think maybe you modern girls need things like your blogs and your Facepages or what-have-you to keep from losing your minds."

Papaw had gotten up and eased his way over to the grill, which now exhaled another burst of smoke. It cascaded gracefully over me, and I couldn't tell if my eyes stung from the smoke or from tears.

12

The Reply

A FEW DAYS LATER, Joe and I sat in the front yard while the kids played, trying to figure out how our three-bedroom house was going to accommodate another baby. We had no extra space like a basement or a finished attic, and my vision for how we could make it all work was getting complicated. I ran inside to grab a pen and paper to draw a diagram for Joe.

I dashed past my laptop, which was in its usual spot on top of our gas-only fireplace. Instead of a chimney, there was a large, flat surface that classy people would have used for decorative items, but we used to collect clutter and as a spot for my computer.

I vaguely registered that there were two new emails up on the screen as I zipped by. Then I stopped. I walked backward to the computer as if someone hit rewind.

One was from Ted. The literary agent.

I jumped over to the laptop and opened his note. I read his words, then read them again because I couldn't believe what I read the first time. It wasn't a blow-off. It wasn't even generic well-wishes. He said that the subject of my blog could potentially make an interesting book, and then—I had to read this part three times to make sure I understood—he said that he would like to see a proposal for a manuscript. If it were good, he would be my agent.

I actually stumbled back from the computer as if it had emitted a shockwave. Normally, writers had to spend months, even years, pushing through the painstaking process of sending query letters and racking up rejections. Even after that, many talented people still couldn't find agents. This opportunity was so rare and so unlikely, I was sure I must be misunderstanding something.

Joe startled in his lawn chair when I burst into the front yard. I was sputtering about an email I sent to an agent after I talked to Hallie at the bookstore, which only added to the confusion. I finally calmed down enough to explain:

"Remember how I told you I emailed that literary agent? Just a casual check-in note?"

"Yeah."

"He replied! And not only did he reply, but he said he'd be interested in representing a book if I want to write one! I mean, I'd need to do a proposal first but—"

"What? Are you kidding?" His face registered happy shock. The kids had begun hovering around Joe, begging for snacks (which was the primary way they spent their outdoor play time) so we moved over to another part of the yard.

"So what do I say?" I asked Joe.

"You say yes!"

"But how could that ever work?" I'd told him about the moment I'd had at church recently, and we'd both agreed that we wanted to accept this call we felt to have more children.

"Jen. Come on. A top literary agent just told you he'd like to represent a book by you. You're seriously asking what you should say?"

"But there are real issues to consider here." I pointed out that, if I said yes to Ted, I would be launching a writing career now, or at least trying. I knew from my previous interactions with this agent that he didn't work with dilettantes. Not only would I have to write an entire manuscript, but I would need to take my blogging work more seriously, too, since modern publishers want to see authors who are actively practicing the craft. On top of that, I probably wouldn't make any money from it for a long time; in fact, there was a real risk that I'd write a book that nobody would publish, and I'd see no income from it at all.

I drew in a long, deep breath. A summer thunderstorm had come through the day before, and the air felt clear and full of possibilities. Could I really take this opportunity? Sure, Joe said I should do it, but he didn't regularly spend hours agonizing about his philosophical stance on the ideal parent/child relationship, so his opinion was suspect.

Since the moment I found out I was expecting my first child, I had been living in the tension between duty and passion. My desire to be a good mother came from the innermost part of my soul, that sacred space where our purest truths reside. Yet it was in that same primal place that I sensed that this work that I wanted to do was good, and that I wasn't supposed to put it on hold indefinitely. But these two things were naturally in conflict with one another . . . weren't they?

My views had been changing thanks to those great conversations with Hallie and Yaya and Papaw. Now, for the first time, I dared to ask: What if there's no conflict?

What if these things actually go hand-in-hand?

Being part of the creation of new life was an experience of God. Yet I also felt something similar in my work. It astounded me whenever I considered that only the creatures made in the image of the Creator can create. Among all the animals on earth, humans alone have the gift of creativity—and, as people had experienced through the millennia, to use this gift is to experience something of God.

Now I wondered: What if all desires to create—both with children and with work—are, in fact, all pointed in the same direction? What if both are different but complementary ways of getting in touch with the ultimate Source of creativity? What if following your God-given passion is not just okay to do during the baby years, but actually something that has the potential to enhance your whole family's life?

I was so lost in thought that I had to snap myself back into the real world when Joe spoke. "All of your concerns are legit. There are real obstacles that we'll have to overcome. I know that. But I also know this: when a once-in-a-lifetime opportunity falls into your lap, you don't say no."

If we were a more affectionate couple, I would have probably hugged him or grabbed his hand or done whatever it is that touchy feely people do to express appreciation. As it was, I gave him a warm smile.

"Okay, so, logistically, what would that even look like? Where would I find the time? How could I get up the energy?"

Joe looked at me intently, as if he were about to deliver the perfect answer to this conundrum. And he said, "I have no idea."

I laughed. "Well, it sounds like a plan, then. Should I go tell Ted yes and we can figure out the details later?"

"Yes. Tell him you're in."

The Office

THE NEXT STEP WAS TO PUT TOGETHER A PROPOSAL. I wasn't officially Ted's client until he approved the concept and we signed a contract, so I pushed through morning sickness to make that happen. I would have expected the constant nausea and fatigue to hamper my work, yet that's not what happened. Some of my strongest ideas appeared when I felt the worst. In addition to a detailed outline, I also had to write a sample chapter, and it came together on a day when I'd been up with Lucy and had gotten only four hours of sleep the night before. It was as if this kind of work connected me with a part of myself that was beyond the physical—my body was weak, but my soul had never been more alive.

Ted wanted the book to be based on the subject of my blog, and my updates there were mostly focused on spirituality, so I outlined a tale about my own journey of faith. I fleshed out a concept that would be a story, rather than a treatise or a how-to guide.

After I pulled together an outline, I filled out the other information, like my media experience ("none") and my approximate audience size ("I got five comments on my last blog post, and only two were spam"). When it was finished, I sent the proposal to Ted.

And then I waited.

To prevent myself from checking email incessantly, I used the wait to set up a home office. We didn't have a lot of room to spare, but Joe and I agreed that if I were serious about this new step, I needed a serious space in which I could do my work. The small dining room was a perfect location for my desk: it was the front room in the house, with two floor-to-ceiling windows that looked out on the porch. With all the bedrooms upstairs, this would allow me to come and go from my office without waking the kids during their naps.

The next weekend, my dad was in town and he helped Joe move an old desk from my mom's garage into the dining room space. It was a bulky, faux wood piece from the 1980s with none of the sleek style I would have preferred, but the $0 price point was right up my alley. The room already contained oak bookcases that Joe and I had custom ordered when we lived downtown, which added a great literary ambiance to the space. Next I picked up maroon curtains from Walmart that Joe installed over the two windows.

When it was all finished, I stood in the doorway and admired the space. If I had been set up in one of the architecturally stunning tech incubator offices in downtown Austin, I couldn't have been happier with my little personal headquarters. I sensed that exciting things could happen thanks to this room, even if I still had no idea how any of it could be possible.

The next day, just as I finished setting out cereal for breakfast, it came. There was an email from Ted, and it had an attachment. I didn't want to get my hopes up. Maybe he'd attached a picture of himself rolling his eyes and making a thumbs-down gesture. Maybe it was the contact info of a therapist for failed writers. I finally summoned the courage to open it, and, sure enough, it was a contract.

It was now official: I was represented by a literary agent, and I was writing a book.

The schedule I created was perfect. I'd examined our daily routine to find pockets of time when I could write (in the mornings before the kids woke, during naptime, and some on the weekends) and I'd managed to find fifteen hours for the book each week that wouldn't even impact the family! I put it all in an Excel spreadsheet, which was, of course, a sub-spreadsheet of the master sheet which contained the family's daily plan. In the past I'd made schedules with various hubristic goals for a family routine (one actually had "Songs and Circle Time" blocked for an hour each morning). My success rate for keeping up with any of them for more than a day was about zero percent, but now I was motivated. If this book were going to get written, I would have to bring a new level of discipline to my life.

I printed both schedules. I set mine on my desk next to my computer and posted the family version on the wall in the kitchen with a red thumb tack. The next day, I faced my first challenge: get downstairs without waking the kids up.

I woke at 5:15 a.m. I moved with the slow, fluid motions of a veteran ninja as I crept toward my bedroom door, which was only feet away from the kids' rooms. It took a full eight seconds for me to ease the door open, then another eight to shut it. But right at the end I got sloppy. I let go of the handle a millisecond too quickly, and when the latch popped back in place a *CLICK!* echoed through the upstairs. I froze, bracing myself for the soul-crushing sound of a child who had been awakened. Nothing. Delighted but cautious, I reached the bottom of the stairs with joyous relief.

And then I heard it.

At first I thought it was a siren from a nearby road. But it got louder and louder, until I realized it was right here, and it wasn't a siren at all. It was Lucy, crying upstairs. I bolted like a madwoman to get to her before she woke Donnell and Lane, but it was too late. By the time I got back upstairs they were all crying. I hauled each of them downstairs, one at a time like a Sherpa, and gathered my sad little crew on the couch. I made gentle shushing sounds and reminded everyone that we use our words when we're upset. When that didn't work, I gave up and turned on a movie.

The next day an afternoon work session was derailed when the doorbell rang and woke the kids. Whoever was there had left by the time I answered the door, which was probably best for everyone.

On Friday, I was determined to get back on track. During nap time, I had just opened my laptop when I saw an elegant figure moving up the walkway: my mother. I flew across the room like Spiderman so that I could let her in before she could knock and wake the kids. I opened the door, then flopped back into my chair.

"Here are the office supplies you wanted for the new desk," she said, holding up a white plastic bag. When she took a good look at me, she added, "Oh, Jenny, you look tired!"

"I am," I said flatly.

"The kids are asleep, right? Don't you think you should take a nap?"

"I need to use the time while the kids are down to work on this book."

"About that. Tell me again why you're doing this right now, with so many little ones?" My parents were both mild-mannered people who avoided confrontation, and my mom had always shown respect for my decisions, so her question wasn't judgmental. It was asked out of genuine confusion.

I ran her through the whole explanation about how this was a once-in-a-lifetime opportunity, though I left out the spiritual stuff about how I felt like I was seeking God through both writing and family. My parents were supportive of our conversions but not really into religious chitchat. Thanks to my exhaustion, when I described this book deal I sounded about as excited as a doctor describing the procedure for a colonoscopy.

She nodded as if she were trying to follow along but didn't quite get all of my reasoning, which wasn't surprising given her vastly different experience of parenthood and, really, of life. My mom was simply *pleasant*—in every way possible. She was pleasant to look at, with a beautiful face, thick, auburn hair, and a complexion that left her perpetually looking at least a decade younger than she actually was. She dressed tastefully and, thanks to her work running the finances for an eye care corporation, she had a never-ending supply of stylish glasses from luxury brands. She didn't drink coffee and rarely had alcohol, yet she had a preternatural ability to be content in almost any situation.

My mom brought this same even-keeled pleasantness to her experience of parenting. She and my dad weren't planning to have kids, but she rolled with it when I came along. She enjoyed pregnancy, then enjoyed staying home with me, and then, when I was seven, went back to work. As far as I could tell, she didn't analyze each decision from twenty different angles. It was as if God took all the neurotic behavior he was planning to give to both of us and sprinkled it all on me.

And so I didn't expect her to fully understand the grand drama that had been playing out in my head over the past few months. To her credit, she did try.

"It makes sense that this is important to you, but couldn't you wait until this new baby gets here and is a little older?"

I dodged the question. All of our parents thought we were crazy for our childbearing choices. They loved each grandchild endlessly, but each had expressed concern about what seemed to be our complete disregard for the entire concept of family planning. I didn't think anyone but Joe was ready to hear about my recent moment at church when I came to peace with our call to have a big family. "Look, it's a long story, but this is just something that's really important to me right now."

My mom nodded, understanding my real point, which was that I wanted to get back to work. She picked up her purse, a dyed blue leather mini duffel, and fished out sunglasses with matching blue frames. "I get it, Jenny. I'm just worried about you. I worry that you're pushing yourself too hard."

I puffed out a breath of air. "I'll try not to."

We exchanged polite goodbyes, and she hadn't even shut the front door before I turned back to my computer screen.

14

Houston, We Have a Problem

JOE SAID WE NEEDED TO TALK AGAIN. I could guess from his tone that it was bad and had to do with money, so I did my best to make the situation as pleasant as possible. I planned for a two-dinner night: an early dinner for the kids and a later dinner for the adults.

I'd been watching a TV series about nineteenth-century British aristocracy and delighted in the concept that young children only joined the family table when they were old enough to behave themselves. If they were still at an age when, say, they would sit in their booster chairs and howl for ten minutes because you allowed the peas to touch the rice on their plate, they ate with the governess in the nursery. That was the life for me. I tried to imagine how we could recreate this in our own house, thinking that if I could just find a governess who would work for free and didn't mind sleeping in the pantry, this could totally happen.

Tonight's kids' meal would be simple hot dogs and green beans, but I planned something more special for Joe and me. I searched around the blog world for favorite date night dinners and found a recipe for bacon-wrapped chicken that looked delicious. I called him as I slid the dish into the oven and told him to get ready to smell something amazing when he got home.

What actually happened when Joe got home was that he walked in the front door to be engulfed by a cascade of smoke. From inside he heard the discordant beeping of every smoke alarm in the house going off at once, mixed with the excited squeals and screams of the kids. "What happened?" he asked, a bit stunned as he tried to process the situation.

"I'm trying a new recipe!" I shouted over the alarms as I waved away plumes of smoke.

He joined me next to the open oven, and we peered in together. The casserole dish I'd filled with high-quality meat products now looked like a pulsating blob that was somehow both liquefied and on fire.

"I found it on a blog," I said.

Joe shut the oven and looked at me in bewilderment, the electronic chorus of the alarms still howling in the background.

"Why would you try a recipe from some blogger you don't even know when you own tons of great cookbooks?"

I brushed off his silly man-question and opened the freezer to hunt for a pizza. Even after we stopped the smoke alarms, fed the kids, and got them in bed, a smoky fog still hung in the air downstairs. Through this haze and over plates of pizza, Joe told me what he'd wanted to talk about.

"Would you ever consider moving to Houston or Dallas?" he asked.

"No."

He laughed. "Well, that was quick."

"Nothing against either city. I've lived in both of them and like both of them, but Austin is our home. I have no interest in moving."

Joe shifted in his seat, obviously about to say something that he'd been thinking over for a long time.

"Here's the problem. It would be so much easier for me to make a living if we were in a bigger city." His research revealed that the number of lawyers per capita in Austin was extraordinarily high (which explained why we knew multiple people in this town who waited tables after graduating from law school). On top of that, he explained, his network here was weak. He'd graduated law school in New York, and his first years as an attorney were spent in Manhattan. His detour into the tech world had cooled his connections in law, so when he'd gone back into this profession three years before, he was essentially starting over.

"A lot of people I know from law school and business school have ended up in Dallas or Houston. They'd be a great source of referrals to help me build my book of business." He had recently talked to an attorney friend who set up shop in Houston and reported booming legal work there. "And housing costs are lower there, too."

There were options in Austin that would help us make ends meet; the problem was that they all involved working at firms with high-pressure environments, where late-night and weekend workdays were a normal part of the culture. Joe had done a lot of searching and had not been able to find an opportunity here in town that would bring in more money and allow him to be a regular presence in the kids' lives. Evidently, that would be different in a bigger city.

I wanted to be open to whatever we needed to do as a family, but I didn't want to move. I'd attended seven schools by the time I was in ninth grade; I felt like I had reached my lifetime limit of starting over in a new place. I had graduated college and begun my career in Austin because it was home. My dad's family had lived here since the 1850s, my grandfather lived here, and I'd always felt nourished by the sense of connection I had to this area.

"I get it that there are more opportunities in bigger cities," I said. "But I really don't think that's the right solution."

As soon as I said it, I wondered: Was I being too stubborn? When I imagined Joe bringing in a better salary for the same (or even less) work, I wasn't as confident of my stance. Joe fumbled aimlessly with a pen, which he'd picked up from a sheet of paper he'd brought to the table. He'd obviously expected this to be a more extensive discussion involving notes. He pushed away his untouched slice of pizza and absentmindedly tapped the pen on the paper.

"Okay, I agree. I don't want to pick up and move to a new city either. But if we keep having kids, with all the expenses that come with that, I doubt we'll have a choice."

Though some authors get advance payments from publishers to live on while they work on their manuscripts, Ted suggested we take a different approach: I would write the entire book before we looked for a publisher. This would give me the space to write on a schedule that worked for me, as well as more time to establish myself as a writer. But it meant that I wouldn't see any income from the book until it was published—if we could even find a publisher at all, which was a big *if*.

I wanted to help Joe with income, so I began looking for paid writing work. I put out feelers through my blog connections and ended up with a freelance gig. It was a straightforward project in which I would write about atheism and belief for a company that printed pamphlets for churches, and the payment would cover a full month of groceries.

I recommitted to the writing schedule that hung from the red tack in the kitchen. The first afternoon, I was about ten minutes into my work when I heard:

DING-DONG-DING-DONG-DING-DONG!

In contrast to the stillness that had filled the house before, the doorbell was an aggressive attack of noise. Worse, the box that made the sound was right outside of the kids' rooms. I sprung from my chair and ran for the door.

DING-DONG-DING-DONG-DING-DONG-DING-DONG-DING-DONG!

I knew who this was. I hadn't seen anyone approach from the office window, so whoever it was had intentionally avoided my view. And most people would not ring the doorbell that aggressively.

This was the neighborhood kids.

Around the time I'd started setting goals for writing time, a group of local hooligans decided to target me for the age-old game of Ding Dong Ditch. This had been happening about once a week—and, even worse, the time these kids got home from school was exactly the time that my kids were down for naps.

I threw open the door. Sure enough, the porch was empty. A slow wind carried over the distant sound of giggles. I stepped forward and looked left, then whipped my head around in confusion when the sound seemed to be coming from the opposite direction. This appeared to amuse whoever was watching me from their hidden location, and as I twirled around again I heard a new burst of muffled laughter. Now that I knew I was being watched, I was suddenly conscious of how dumpy I felt. My maternity jeans were too tight, and the old t-shirt I'd chosen from a pile on the closet floor was wrinkled and faded, its once-black color now a mottled dark gray.

I slunk back inside just as the sounds of more snickers floated my way. I wondered if I'd been targeted because I seemed like a creepy recluse to these kids. The houses on our block were close together, separated by not even twenty feet of space, so I had plenty of neighbors on this street. Yet I knew the names of only three of them. I was evidently a shadowy figure whose existence was so mysterious that it attracted the attention of local bullies.

As I leaned on the closed door to catch my breath, I heard the sounds of someone calling me from upstairs. The doorbell had woken up Donnell. Then I heard a wail. Lucy. A second later, Lane's voice joined the mix. No more writing time today. With four hours until Joe got home, I stretched out on the couch in defeat and let the kids run around in the living room.

On the end table was a stack of stapled papers I'd been meaning to read. It was a series of interviews with accomplished authors and creativity experts about how to excel at your craft. I pulled the papers onto the couch and began reading.

The first tip was from a famous memoirist, who said that the key to becoming a great writer is to have a predictable writing schedule. Lucy began hitting me while demanding a new bottle of apple juice, and she smacked the paper out of my hands in the process. I told her to hold on for a second, picked up the printout, and kept reading. The tips continued:

You must get plenty of quality sleep in order to do your best work.
Write every day at the same time.
Avoid all distractions.
Consistency is key! Hit your word counts every day.

I owned a stack of books on similar subjects—writing, creativity, following your passions—and they all had similar messages. The more I read, the more I got the impression that writing and any other creative work could only take place in a controlled, predictable life.

I rolled onto my back and stared at the ceiling, listening to Donnell and Lane play a game in which one of them was a puppy and the other was a scorpion (which reminded me to call the exterminator). This doorbell ringing issue was perhaps the most annoying interruption to my schedule, but the reality was that I never seemed to get the time I needed to do my work the right way.

15

BFFs

SO I WENT INTO TRY-HARDER BATTLE MODE. I committed to getting out of bed as soon as my alarm went off to maximize morning writing time. I got a noisier fan to put outside the bedrooms. It sounded like a Category 3 hurricane was perpetually hovering over the hallway, but I sure could make it downstairs without waking the kids. I pushed my hour of evening writing time to two hours, which meant less sleep but more progress.

The editor at the pamphlet company mentioned that if everything went well with this project, there would be more work in the future. I was typing away one afternoon, lost in the fun of taking a jumble of thoughts and channeling them into a clear stream of words, when a familiar noise exploded through the house:

DING-DONG-DING-DONG-DING-DONG-DING-DONG!

I scrambled to the window and threw back the curtains. For the first time, I got a look at the group, at least the backs of them. There were four of them, all girls. I pounded on the glass and shouted for them to cut it out, but they only glanced over their shoulders before running around the corner. Just as I lost sight of them, the sounds of crying floated down from upstairs. I stared at the spot on the sidewalk where I'd last seen them, wishing I had a superpower to shoot lasers from my eyes and zap people from afar.

My mind was ablaze with anger. And then, suddenly, it was cooled when a fresh, peaceful thought glided into my mind:

You should reach out to them.

It seemed to be one of those ideas inspired by God, since it definitely did not come from me. I tried to reject this bizarre message, but I couldn't escape the sense that these kids might have been sent to my door for a reason other than testing my anger management abilities. I had a strange feeling that they would continue ringing my doorbell until I let them in, one way or another. So I disconnected the doorbell.

Whatever cosmic forces were sending these neighborhood miscreants my way, I would show them all by making this a non-issue. I gave now-wide-awake Donnell, Lane, and Lucy cookies to keep them happy for a few moments while I got to work. I stood on a stool, removed the plastic cover from the doorbell box on the wall, and carefully unwound the wire connected to the bell.

In the days that followed, it was with unadulterated joy that I listened to the scampering on the front porch, confused whispers, then the sound of retreating footsteps. I had taken my writing time back and defeated the neighborhood punks! It felt good to win at life again.

The next day, my kids were toddling around the front yard and had been given their five-minute warning that it was time go inside. I kept pulling my phone out of my pocket to glance at the time, making sure everything proceeded according to plan. Then Donnell's voice cried, "Mommy, a bird! He's hurt!"

I ran over to see a small bird who was flailing in the grass. I was trying to figure out what to do when Lucy crawled too close to Lane, and Lane tripped over her, which knocked them both into Donnell. Before I knew it, everyone was crying and I had no bandwidth to help this poor injured animal.

It was time for God and me to have a serious chat.

Listen, Lord, I said in my best we-need-to-talk voice. *There is a lot of craziness in this house. We are not perfect people, in case you haven't noticed. But please don't let this be the kind of house where birds die on my lawn because I have my hands too full to take care of them.*

And then I did something I always hated to do: I asked for

help. I always wanted God to answer every prayer by beaming down the ability for me to conquer all adversity on my own, but it was pretty clear that that's not what was going to happen here. So I ended the prayer by saying, *I want to help this bird, but I can't do this on my own. Please send help.*

Almost immediately, the doorbell ringers appeared.

They were headed from one end of the street to the other, and their trajectory would take them right past my house. My gaze briefly met with theirs, but we all looked away. The bird flipped over as it struggled at my feet. They were getting close. I couldn't do this alone. But every time I looked at them I could only think of all the afternoons they'd ruined for me.

They walked in front of the house, staying safely on the other side of the street, studiously avoiding looking my direction. It was about to be too late. Just before they drifted out of earshot, I gulped hard. I forced myself to shout, "Hey! Girls! I need help!"

They paused and examined the situation with apprehension, perhaps assuming that this was a trap where I would finally enact my vengeance.

"There's a bird here," I explained. "He's injured."

Hesitantly, they approached my spot in the driveway. When they saw that there was indeed a small bird in front of me, they picked up speed. When they got to us, I saw that they were much younger than I'd guessed, one of them probably only eight years old.

"Aaaw, poor thing! What happened?" the youngest one asked.

"I don't know. It looks like its wing is injured." Lucy and Lane were fighting again, but I shushed them so I could talk. "I'm Jennifer, by the way."

"Hi, I'm Carmen. This is my sister, Megan."

"I'm Riley."

"I'm Sophia."

An awkward silence filled the air as we all anticipated that the next statement would be to acknowledge that we already knew one another. I changed the subject. "So does anyone know how to help this bird? As you can see, I have my hands full."

"We could take it back to our house and try to help it. Poor little guy!" Carmen said. "Do you have a box we could put him in?"

I tried to set Lucy down so I could dig through the shelves in the garage, but she acted as if I were lowering her into molten lava. I froze in frustration, and then Megan appeared at my side.

"Hey there, you want to come with me?" her smile was so innocent and bright that Lucy happily went into her arms.

I emerged with a box a few minutes later, as well as gardening gloves to pick up the bird. When the animal was all set, Carmen ran off with it to see if her older brother could help with its care. I expected the others to leave too, but they stayed. We chatted about where they went to school and what classes they loved and hated. When I finally announced that I had to get back to work, they seemed reluctant to leave.

My writing schedule was demolished that day due to my work as bird rescuer. Part of me was silently screaming in frustration, but I admonished myself to chill out and make up for lost time tomorrow. When nap time rolled around the next day, my whole body tingled with excitement. When I took my place behind my desk I actually rubbed my hands together in anticipation, like a madman in a movie. I cracked my knuckles to prepare my hands for the awesomeness that was about to flow from my fingers, and then . . .

KNOCK-KNOCK-KNOCK!

I looked out the office window to see the neighbor girls congregating on my porch, this time not hiding from my view. They could see me through a space in the curtains and were waving. They weren't running.

I stifled an exasperated sigh and went to greet them. I stood in the entryway with the door cracked as little as possible, displaying the same posture I used when the Jehovah's Witnesses came by.

"Hi, girls, good to see you," I said thinly.

"We wanted to update you on the bird!" Riley, the youngest one of the group, announced.

"He's doing better," Carmen said. "My mom says she thinks he's going to make it."

"Oh, that's great. I'm happy to hear it." I put my hand on the door in preparation for closing it.

They just stood there. There was a long silence while I waited for them to say goodbye, and they waited for . . . something else. When I couldn't take the awkwardness any longer, I finally said what they were evidently hoping I would say: "Do you want to come in?"

They twittered excitedly. One of them did a little jump.

"Yes! Sure!" Megan said.

With my back to them as I led everyone into the kitchen, I checked the clock on the stove. On a good day, my kids might nap for two hours. If I could get these girls out in thirty minutes, I'd still have a solid chunk of time left for my work. I offered them seats at the table, moving Lucy's high chair and pulling in my office chair so that everyone had a place.

"You want something to drink?" I asked. "I just bought this new orange tea." They all responded with enthusiastic yeses, just as I realized that I had no clean mugs. The glass-fronted cabinet by the end of the table caught my eye. Our gleaming white wedding china sat there, never touched. We always said we'd get it out for "special occasions," but we never seemed to find an occasion quite special enough. I looked from the cabinet to the girls, their faces open and giddy. I decided to go for it.

Each girl got a tea cup and saucer, the snow-white china lined with a simple silver pattern that was still shiny. I lifted a large serving bowl from its place in the display case and dumped in a family-sized bag of pretzels.

I set the bowl on the table in front of them. And then I didn't know what to do.

There are lots of people in the world who naturally gravitate to kids, for whom having a gaggle of pre-teen girls in their kitchen would be a normal activity. I was not one of those people. If I had found myself in a kitchen full of trained circus bears, I couldn't have felt any less at ease. I stood awkwardly next to the sink, trying to think of what to say or what I could offer them next.

"Miss Jennifer, are you Catholic?" Carmen asked, looking at the Christ the Teacher icon above the couch. Which, now that I looked at it, had something—was that peanut butter?—smudged on the bottom of the frame.

"Yes," I said, wondering why she asked. "Are you?"

"No, but my uncle knows some Catholics, and they kind of got him in trouble a while back."

"Why?"

"Have you heard of the thing of burying a statue of St. Joseph in your yard if you want to sell your house?"

"Yes . . ." I said, not sure where she was going with this. It was an informal tradition that I'd seen a few Catholics do, usually while wrestling with whether or not they were being superstitious. Catholic bookstores sometimes sold tiny St. Joseph figurines for that purpose.

"Well, everyone told my uncle that it worked really well, but he's not like Catholic or anything, so he didn't know how to do it right. He found this big statue of Saint Joseph that was about as tall as I am, and he buried that in his yard one night. But the neighbors saw him doing it, and it looked like he was burying a body, so they called the cops on him."

A laugh burst from my lungs that was so big and so unexpected that it shattered all the pent-up awkwardness within me. Still laughing, I moved to the table and eased into a seat. "Are you serious? He did *what*?"

The conversation was now cracked open, and waves of laughter and giggles rolled over the sounds of chatter and clinking china. The girls were so excited that they kept jumping up and raising their hands and exclaiming, "Miss Jennifer, pick me! Pick me!" When I learned that some of them had surprisingly serious stresses in their lives, I felt like pretty much the worst human being in the world for all the things I'd thought about them back when they were ringing the doorbell.

They eventually announced that they had to go. On the way out, Riley paused at the door. She turned back, her brown eyes meeting mine hopefully.

"Miss Jennifer, can we all be BFFs?" she asked.

"BFFs?" I'd heard the term but it didn't register immediately.

"Best Friends Forever."

My throat was so tight I could barely choke out a "yes."

16

No Freaking Out

WITH ONLY WEEKS BEFORE THE BABY ARRIVED, I scrambled to hire a temporary babysitter. We had to dig into savings to cover this expense, but Joe reminded me of what we'd both learned from the tech startup world: sometimes you have to invest money to make money. There are always startup costs for any business, even the "business" of a simple freelance writing career. If you believe in your idea, it's worth the risk of some capital. I wouldn't be able to keep a sitter over the long term, but I figured that this might be what I needed to get my schedule back on track.

The next day I set to work on an ad. When it was finished, I called Joe at work to share it with him.

"Here's what I have: 'Busy family with three children ages four, two, and one needs a babysitter for the month of February. No experience necessary, just a positive attitude!'"

The phone was quiet for a moment. "You're making it sound like they don't have to do anything with this job."

That was true. As usual, I was trading in the currency of good vibes. If it were up to me, I would have also mentioned that I'd double their pay if they smiled a lot and pretended to like me.

"Tell you what," he said. "Why don't I take a stab at the draft and send it back to you?"

I agreed. Within the hour, Lawyer Joe had crafted a page-long job description that covered every possible task we might ever want completed. It read like a script for one of those limit-testing reality shows where contestants have to eat cockroaches. We agreed on some major edits to soften the tone, and I typed it all up and posted it online.

I'd been through this process before, when Donnell was a baby and I was helping Joe set up his law firm. The girl we found was a bright college student from Pakistan, and she was a joy to have in the house. She was a devout Muslim who taught Donnell words in Urdu, and watching her observe Ramadan made me feel a whole lot better about giving up ice cream during Lent. I really hoped we could find someone like her again.

I shouldn't have been surprised when we didn't get many applicants. Of the ones who sent cover letters more detailed than "WHERE U LIVE?", I selected the few who seemed decent and suggested we meet at a coffee shop. Two didn't show up, another had misunderstood the job as a pet sitting gig, and one seemed okay. I decided to do a second interview with the okay one, a woman named Terri. She was an empty-nester whose child was now a successful businesswoman, and she was looking for a part-time job to beef up her retirement account.

I couldn't escape the feeling that she disliked me. At our first meeting, she sunk into her chair next to the barista stand, occasionally huffing and taking long breaths, as if whatever question I had just asked had vaporized her life force. She asked me pointed questions about the way I ran my home and frowned or raised her eyebrows at most of my answers. But I did get the feeling that the kids would be safe with her, so I invited her to visit the house for a second interview.

When I saw her walk down the driveway the next day, I hoped fervently that I'd misremembered her demeanor, that maybe she wouldn't greet me again with that facial expression like she'd stepped on gum on a hot day. It was not to be. The kids had gotten into a fight just before she arrived, and they were all whining or crying when she walked in. In order for us to talk, I silenced them by giving Donnell a cracker and handing the two girls bottles of juice.

I turned to Terri to begin our conversation, but she spoke first.

"She still uses a bottle?" she said, her face registering genuine shock as she stared at two-and-a-half-year-old Lane.

"Oh, no, she doesn't. Only when we have guests over," I said, which was a lie in addition to making no sense. The reality was that keeping up with the Academy of Pediatrics' standards for when children should give up pacifiers and bottles was number 4,318 on my list of life priorities right now, but I needed to pretend like I cared.

"I just can't believe you have another one on the way," she said as I began to show her around. She'd already made that comment twice at the coffee shop meeting, and yet I still hadn't been able to think of a more clever reply than to laugh nervously.

I walked her through the house, which was an opportunity to remember that I hadn't cleaned the kids' rooms or emptied the diaper trash can in days. When I opened the door to my room, I immediately regretted it. Piles and piles of unfolded laundry made it look like a shot from one of those hoarder intervention shows, and then there was something else: in the corner of the room sat a box of junk we kept meaning to put away, and right on top was the beer bong. We'd taken it from the sandbox to put back with Joe's other fraternity mementos but never got around to dealing with it. I wasn't sure if she saw it, but if she did, it probably all made sense to her now: we clearly had this kind of life because we were main-lining gallons of alcohol directly into our stomachs in our bedroom every night.

I shut the door and prepared to move on to the bathroom, but she didn't follow me. When I turned to check on her, she was standing with her arms folded.

"Are you staying in this house?"

"Excuse me?"

"This house. This is it? Aren't you getting a bigger house?"

She looked around my home with such pure disapproval that I suddenly saw it differently myself. Before that moment, I had

had a deep affection for this house, even with all its mess. We had discovered it accidentally during a difficult time in our lives. After we left our downtown condo we'd moved in with my mom while Joe changed careers. When Lane was born we knew we needed a place of our own, but we couldn't afford it. I said an impossible prayer that we might find a place to live, and shortly after that a road construction detour sent us by this house. There was a *For Sale by Owner* sign in the front yard, put up only hours before. We would find out that he was anxious to sell since he'd gotten a new job out of town. We ended up getting it at such a good price that the mortgage company required a sworn affidavit saying that we had no previous relationship with the seller.

I'd always considered this house to be one of the greatest answered prayers of my life. But now, seeing it through Terri's eyes, it seemed small and cheap. Even though I had felt so confident about our life choices in the months since I saw that big family outside of the church, I now second-guessed it all as if reviewing a decision I made while intoxicated. What were we doing cramming all of these kids into a small house? What kind of childhood was that?

My posture deflated as we walked back down the stairs, and I didn't even try to seem energetic. When we paused by the front door, I said, "So, do you want the job?"

She took a big breath as she examined the entryway with the shoes and jackets scattered on the floor. Finally, she huffed out the air. "I guess. Sure."

Terri's first and second days on the job went as well as expected, which is to say that they were disastrous but I wasn't surprised. While changing a diaper she'd think aloud about how differently she'd done things when she raised her daughter. She didn't ask about our rules or routines but ran the house with her own ideas about how to raise children—which, admittedly, involved a lot higher standards than mine. This led to no end of conflicts with the kids, who were baffled by concepts like not snacking in between meals and putting shoes on before going outside. I knew I should probably step in to help her understand the way we did things, but I lost my nerve every time I thought about speaking up.

Instead, I cowered in my office, trying in vain to get work done. The pamphlet company had sent me a second project, and I hoped it was a sign that there would be many more to come. I managed to dash out the text and turn it in, but I stalled out after that. I spent most of my babysitter time surfing the web nervously, wondering if I should intervene in the various awkward situations I heard playing out between Terri and the kids. At one point I got an email from Joe with the subject: *Remember that you are supposed to enjoy your time while the sitter is there. No freaking out!* I deleted it and went back to freaking out.

On the third day of her employment, I was thumbing through a printout of my book manuscript when I heard Terri shout from the living room: "GET OFF! GET OFF OF THERE NOW!"

I threw the papers aside and jumped to my feet. She hadn't raised her voice with the kids before, so she was clearly at a breaking point. Each day she'd seemed more and more like a zoo employee who signed up for the butterfly exhibit but got locked in the cage with the howler monkeys.

I burst into the living room to see that Donnell and Lane were standing on the couch, staring at Terri as if she were shouting at them in Japanese. As if to herald my arrival, the cartoon channel started playing the *Jabberjaw* song—the one by Hallie's husband's old band. *Me and my friends get no respect / What does Scooby do that we neglect?* Dan crooned over a happy chorus of punk guitar riffs and trombones. Normally the song filled me with grateful thoughts about my friendship with Hallie, but now it barely registered.

"It's the Jabba Jaw song!" Donnell announced. He and Lane resumed jumping on the couch. Lucy bounced up and down, squealing in excitement. I held up my hand and did my death-ray mom stare to convey *NOT NOW*, which was ignored by all.

Terri turned to me, her eyes burning with indignation. "Donnell told me that you allow your children to jump on the furniture. Is this true?"

Words caught in my throat. The honest answer was that I'd never thought much about it. There were no rules against such a thing in my own house when I was growing up, but that was only because I was a docile kid who avoided anything that resembled exercise, so my parents never needed to make that provision. They'd had to create a Byzantine rules system around how late I could stay up, how much time I could spend on the computer, and what books I was allowed to read. But there was no need to set parameters around my physical movement since there was so little of it. I was a stranger in a strange land when it came to parenting, and this constantly left me caught off guard by these sorts of questions that were second nature to other people.

Part of me wanted to go ahead and green-light the couch jumping. Since we were cooped up in the house all day, maybe it was a good way for them to get exercise. Maybe I could say that my living room was an indoor playground for minimalists, where the couch did double-duty as a piece of furniture and a trampoline. Certainly there was no worry of making the stained, tattered object look any worse than it already was.

My hesitation was the only answer Terri needed.

"This isn't working, Jennifer."

I nodded stiffly. The refrain came again from the television: *Me and my friends get no respect!*

"I can't do this anymore. I just . . . This is over. I quit."

"I understand," I said. I knew she was going to say it, so my face showed no surprise. I grabbed our checkbook from the kitchen counter and wrote out her full payment through the end of the week. I never realized how long it takes to fill out all the information on a check until I had Terri standing there and glaring at me, the kids jumping on the couch to the *Jabberjaw* song in the background.

Terri snatched the check from my fingers and turned to march toward the door. She stopped after one step, then turned back to me.

"I don't know what it is you've been working on while I'm here . . ."

"I'm writing a book," I interjected. Out of habit, my voice became light and happy when I spoke of it. "It's this thing, something I've always wanted to do. I had this chance—"

"Really?" she interrupted me. It seemed only to deepen her disapproval now that I'd revealed that this work I was doing wasn't even a real job. "You really think that's what you should be doing with your time right now?" she said, looking at my hugely pregnant stomach.

I fumbled for an answer, but she held up her hand to indicate that none was needed. "Forget it. It's none of my business," she said and turned to leave.

17

The Farmer's Wife

"AT LEAST YOU HAD A GOOD SOUNDTRACK for the most humiliating moment of your life," Hallie said when I called her to rehash the Terripocalypse.

I refused to laugh. "Stop. I'm trying to have an existential crisis."

Inexplicably, my day had actually gotten worse after Terri quit. The editor at the pamphlet publisher had called and said that my new piece was completely in the wrong direction. I was so distracted by the morning's events that I couldn't figure out how to get on the same page with him, and we ended up agreeing to cancel the project altogether.

"So what are you going to do now that you don't have a babysitter?" Hallie asked.

"I have no idea," I said. That morning I had tried to use the kids' quiet time to send out new queries about paying work. It ended abruptly when I heard Donnell announce, "Mommy says we can't play with those pens," and I ran out to see Lucy wielding a Sharpie that had already been used to decorate a wall near the back door. I was obviously frustrated, so to cheer me up Donnell drew a special picture for me. Its title was *I Love Mommy* and it featured two colorful blobs under what appeared to be a sun (I was the blob on the left). I flipped it over to see that it was drawn on the back of my writing schedule that had been secured by the red tack in the kitchen.

On top of my endless failures getting time for work, my due date was near. When this baby arrived I would have four children under age five, three of them in diapers. When I thought about what life would look like here in a few short weeks, I became filled with a numb dread. I could count on being woken up every two hours, around the clock, for the foreseeable future. Despite sessions with multiple midwives and lactation consultants, nursing was always excruciatingly painful for the first few weeks. Our babies often had bouts of colic, which meant days of inexplicable fussing and crying.

I shook my head when I thought of it all. What was I thinking? No wonder Terri was so baffled by my choices. She could have worked on her delivery, but maybe she was right. I had set out on this adventure with dreams of thriving both as a mother and as a writer; currently, I was failing at both.

Late that evening, I sat in bed with my laptop open next to me as I prepared a blood-thinner shot. I was looking over my book wish list while I tapped the syringe and pushed out the air bubble. Lately I'd been devouring classic true survival stories like *Endurance* and *Adrift*. It gave me a healthy sense of perspective to remember that no matter what went wrong in my day, at least I wasn't floating on a rubber raft in the middle of the Atlantic, where a great white shark could emerge from the abyss and swallow me whole at any moment.

I had just finished the shot when an email popped up. With my stomach still burning as if I'd had a brush with a glowing-hot poker, I opened the message. It was from another woman who had a blog, a Canadian farmer's wife named Ann ("just plain 'Ann,' without even the fanciful *e*," she often said). Around the time Lucy was born, we had struck up an email friendship over our faith and mutual love of writing. When she encountered technical issues setting up a new domain name for her site, I'd offered to help. I valued her friendship for a lot of reasons, but the main one was that she seemed to be a person who had a deep and genuine relationship with God. I knew from our earliest correspondence that she was someone from whom I could learn a lot about what it looked like to have a clue.

And so I sat up in bed when I saw that she was emailing me about the book I was writing. I'd recently announced the project on my blog, and she said she had some private news to share along those lines.

Ann confided that she, too, had recently signed a contract to write a book. She hadn't told many people yet, but she wanted to reach out since we were in the same boat. She was a homeschooling mother of six kids, in addition to her responsibilities around the farm, and she was struggling to balance it all.

"I too have *no idea* how to do this while living with six children twenty-four hours a day, faithfully educating and feeding and caring for these kids," she said in her note. Her words were as kind and as warm as if she'd been here in person to put her arm around me (which would have caused me to stiffen awkwardly since I never knew how to react to physical affection, so maybe it was better that we were doing this by email).

The fact that someone like her was facing these same concerns was so comforting that I forgot about the pain from the shot. Sometimes you don't even feel a burden while you're carrying it, and you only know its weight once it's removed, in the lightness you experience in its absence. I hadn't even realized how wearying it was to believe that I was the only person crazy enough to get myself into this position.

I wrote her back to express my gratitude at receiving her note, and she had some specific words of encouragement for me: "We will labor. We will keep the end in view: His glory in all things. We will struggle. But it will be in HIS energy. His energy that we pray and trust and believe is powerfully at work in us," her note continued. "I take this verse, Colossians 1:29, and give it to you: 'To this end I labor, struggling with all His energy, which so powerfully works in me.'" Just that morning Hallie and I had been cheering one another up by sending funny, slightly vulgar memes we'd found on the internet. I made a mental note to tell her that we should really include more Bible verses in our emails.

Ann concluded: "As I stumble and fumble through this, (I am scared, weak—and tremble, fear I'm too spiritually impoverished to rise to the task He's given) I just wanted you to know: I will pray for you. That God will give even thirty minutes a day, a hundred words here, a hundred words there. In Him, all things are possible—even a wee little bit at a time. He'll make it clear what you are to do. He's gifted you and opened doors and He alone will give clarity on the direction for this season."

I closed the laptop and set it aside, then switched off my bedside lamp. The heat clicked on, the warm air flowing from the vent above me like breath in the darkness. I leaned back against the headboard and closed my eyes. I said I believed in God now—that was, in fact, the main subject of this book I was working on. I said that a desire to have a deeper connection to the ultimate Creator was a driving force behind this process. And yet none of that came through in my current approach. This was a struggle I'd had since the moment I came to faith: the temptation to *act* like I was still an atheist, even though, intellectually, I was a believer. Moving my faith down from my head to my heart, and into my moment-to-moment actions, had never come naturally to me. I certainly hadn't done it when it came to my efforts to balance writing work and family life. And now I suspected that that was a big part of the problem.

The baby arrived on a Monday afternoon in March. Her official name was Catherine, but we called her Kate. And in a stunning turn of events, she was an easy baby—really, really easy. I didn't think that Joe and I had the kind of genes that created laid back children. (We once compared the regions of the world where our various ancestors were from and realized that they were all areas settled by Vikings. At that particular moment Donnell was jumping on the couch wielding a plastic sword while Lane and Lucy hit each other with baby dolls, and suddenly everything made sense.)

But this baby slept four and six hours at a time as soon as we brought her home from the hospital; she slept through the night, twelve hours at a stretch, starting at six weeks. She nursed easily, and, for the first time, it wasn't horrifically painful. If she was woken up, she went back to sleep quickly. When she was awake, she was happy and quiet. Unlike my other children, Kate didn't act as if she were being lowered into a bed of cacti every time I tried to put her down. At one point I took her to the pediatrician and demanded to know what was wrong with this baby that all she did was sleep and smile.

Before her birth, I had invested so much time thinking about how difficult it would be to have an infant in the house (Joe affectionately called this "pre-worrying"). After my initial burst of excitement about following this crazy call to have a big family, I got stressed. I knew that it would all be too much for me to handle, and I'd end up in a special mental ward for mothers who are really bad at family planning. And these mental movies of all the worst-case scenarios were set in a graceless, godless landscape where I would have no assistance, divine or otherwise.

In the countless hours I spent chronicling what might go wrong once this baby arrived, I never paused to think of the *good* things that might happen; I never stopped to imagine joy.

When the baby was only six weeks old, a stomach flu ravaged the house. And this was no ordinary stomach flu; this was a strong, determined virus that left anyone who caught it vomiting so suddenly and forcefully that it looked like something out of a *Saturday Night Live* skit. If I had known this was coming back when I was pregnant, I would have dedicated entire hours out of my day to dreading it.

Yet, when I found myself actually living it, it was a time filled with love and unexpected graces. Joe took the week off from work, and the whole family spent days lying around the living room, watching silly movies and TV shows. Joe and I exchanged wry, commiserating looks as we passed each other in the hallways in the middle of the night, him rushing a kid to the bathroom while I ran downstairs with an armful of soiled sheets. Miraculously, neither the baby nor I caught the bug.

One night, at the height of the illness, we decided at two o'clock in the morning to move everyone into our room. Joe spread out the sleeping bags on the floor, and I brought the kids in one by one. They each went to sleep immediately, and after we finished tucking them in, Joe and I returned to bed ourselves. Only I couldn't sleep. I found myself wanting to stay awake and enjoy this quiet moment when I could sit in complete stillness and listen to the hushed symphony of my children's breaths as they slept.

Baby Kate's crib was next to my side of the bed, and I stood to check on her. Her tiny body was warm in her pink sleep sack, and her fist, which was smaller than a walnut, was curled next to her face. I picked her up and brought her into bed with me; I would have no sooner disturbed one of my other sleeping babies than I'd disturb a sleeping javelina, but I knew she wouldn't stir. I kissed her forehead and watched her eyelashes flutter as she slept.

The seemingly inconvenient timing of this baby's arrival made me feel a special kinship with her, since I myself arrived into the world at an inconvenient time. My parents had not planned to have kids and had spent the first decade of their marriage crafting an exciting, child-free lifestyle. They owned a small, inexpensive plane and often split gas money with friends to fly to an island near their home in Florida, rolling out sleeping bags on the runway to save on hotel costs. They threw legendary parties in which large trash cans were filled with potent punches, and guests ended up literally dancing on tables. They drove a laser blue 1971 Stingray Corvette convertible. Then, after a contraception failure, I came along.

My parents' lives were sent in an entirely different direction. They sold the plane and the sports car and bought a station wagon. It was brown. They threw themselves into family life, both of them showing a dedication as parents that made most people assume that having children had been something they'd desired for years. I smiled at the visual of me and my little bundle there on the bed, her warm, tiny body burrowed against mine. The surprise baby holding the surprise baby.

I'd been reading up on Frances of Rome, the fourteenth-century woman who inspired Kate's middle name. The main thing I knew about Frances was that she was extremely introverted, which endeared her to me. But I had just read about how she, too, did not initially think family life was for her. When she was a young woman she was insistent that a life of quiet contemplation as a nun was the right path for her. She went on to get married and have children, and she threw herself into loving the people God sent into her life to such an extent that she was considered a saint. When her husband fell ill after forty years of marriage, she threw herself into his care. As he lay dying, he turned to her and said, "I feel as if my whole life has been one beautiful dream of purest happiness. God has given me so much in your love."

I felt like there was a message for me here in this story of this woman who learned that her own plan was not always the best plan. With the smell of vomit lingering in the air, I felt like I was going to burst with gratitude for this beautiful dream I was living—not in spite of all the unexpected twists and turns, but because of them.

Poopocalypse

THERE WAS A SAYING THAT JOE AND I ALWAYS HEARD in tech startup circles: "Be wrong as fast as you can." Its meaning was this: If some part of your project—or maybe even the whole thing—is going to fail, it's better to know sooner rather than later. That way you don't pour time and energy into wild goose chases.

I was trying to be wrong as quickly as I could with this writing career. The success or failure of this book project would let us know whether there was any hope of me having long-term, paying work as an author. And we needed an answer on that sooner rather than later because we had some big decisions to make.

The baby was four months old, and we were now a family of six squeezed into a small space. Every day it seemed clearer that we couldn't stay in Austin and live a balanced, family-focused life without an extra source of income. Soon we would need a bigger house, in addition to various other expenses that come with a growing family. Joe simply didn't have that kind of income available to him in the Austin law market—at least not without ramping up into a high-pressure job. The options were clear: make this writing career work or pick up everything and move to a new city.

Per our new baby tradition, we went into what we called Bare-Minimum Mode for the first three months after Kate was born. During this time, we didn't do anything ambitious—and we considered mopping the floor and cooking recipes with more than five ingredients "ambitious." Bare-Minimum Mode was about consciously setting aside goals and plans so that we could rest, recover, and adjust to the new family size.

But now it was time to get back into regular life, and, not surprisingly, I was finding it nearly impossible to get anything at all done. On the one hand, I was trying to bring God into the process beyond just ranting heavenward when things didn't go my way. My friend Ann continued to be a font of wisdom, and I looked forward to every note she sent—in part because each one radiated grace and love, and in part because I was baffled as to how she was able to keep up with her big book contract while homeschooling six kids, and I wanted to know her secret. Also, I just loved the way she wrote. (Her latest note contained the smile-inducing opening, "Just to offer a mixed bouquet of thoughts that I've plucked while cleaning up after lunch . . .")

She constantly encouraged me to trust that God would give me the time I needed. She told me to remember that this would all happen on his timeframe, not mine. It sounded nice, in theory, but I needed to make money. And, in the past month, I'd only written a page and a half of text.

"You want some help?" Hallie asked when I laid all of this out for her.

"You're so sweet. No, thanks."

"Seriously, Jen. I'm excited about what you're doing and would really like to help. Let me come over on Friday. Dan is taking the day off from job hunting so I could watch your kids, do some cleaning for you, whatever you need."

"That is such an awesome offer, but I really couldn't. It's fine. I'll figure something out."

We were about to hang up since she and I both needed to start lunch, when she interrupted our goodbyes. "You know, actually, can I be really honest with you for a sec?"

This sounded ominous. "Umm, sure."

"Do you think there's any chance that God is trying to show you how you might be able to get this project done, and you're not seeing it?"

"What do you mean?"

"I mean just now. I could easily give you a whole afternoon of writing time. I'm happy to. I *want* to! And you turned it down."

There was no way I could let her come over. It was so hard for both of us to leave the house that, though we talked on the phone almost every day, Hallie hadn't been here in three months, maybe four. She couldn't possibly be prepared for what a disaster it was, and she would undoubtedly start looking for a replacement friend as soon as she walked in the door. But I realized that if I turned down this offer of help, I couldn't complain about making no progress on the book this week—and I really wanted to preserve the option of complaining.

"Okay, fine, but don't say I didn't warn you about the state my house is in," I said.

I thought I detected a note of victory in Hallie's voice when she said, "I'll be there at noon."

When Hallie arrived, the neighbor girls were standing on the porch with her, having shown up at the same time. I introduced everyone and said, "Girls, I would love for you to hang out today, but this is a big work day for me so unfortunately I can't."

A brief look of disappointment flashed across their faces. Now that school was out for the summer, they'd been coming by multiple times per week. We'd passed many afternoons lounging around the living room, them and my kids draped across the couch and the floor, chatting and watching shows. Carmen lit up with an idea.

"Oh, can we help while you're working?"

"That is so sweet, but—"

Hallie jumped in. "Yes! What a kind offer. Miss Jen would love your help, girls. Come on in."

Lucy was already down for a nap, I put the baby down for her nap, and the neighbor girls set up a game of Candy Land with

Donnell and Lane on the kitchen table. Hallie started cleaning. It took every fiber of my being not to insist that she stop, but I forced myself to get to work as we'd planned.

I hopped up the stairs to retrieve my laptop from my bedroom, and on the way I ducked into the kids' bathroom to turn out the light. A sharp smell caught my attention, like a diaper in need of changing. Surely not. I looked toward the room where I'd just put Lucy down for a nap.

She hadn't been making noise, which undoubtedly meant she was sound asleep, so I opened the door slowly to peek in. If I had had a thousand years to prepare myself, I would not have been ready for what I saw: Lucy was wide awake, sitting up in her crib, a broad smile on her face. She looked like she'd been rolling in a mud pit.

But it wasn't mud.

It was then that I remembered the number one truth of parenting: *If you think you smelled poop, YOU DID.* My gaze drifted to the scene around her, my eyes glassy and moving slowly like when people are in shock. Evidently, she had eaten something that didn't agree with her and tried to handle the resulting diaper accident herself. It looked like someone had hooked up a fire hose to a latrine and sprayed it around her corner of the room. The mess was everywhere: in her hair, ground into stuffed animal fur, smeared across toys, all over the pillow, and, somehow, also on the wall.

I started shouting. My shouts didn't have any particular action item associated with them. I wasn't asking for assistance, since I knew I was on my own for this one. I wasn't mad at Lucy, since she was only one year old and her actions were a horrifically misguided attempt to help. It was just a loud, primal babbling of despair, peppered with gasps and mumbled profanity. I stepped forward to open the window to let the smell out but stopped when I remembered the child safety locks that entombed us in this room. I started to pick Lucy up, then stopped when I considered my own clothes. In the end I just stood there, frozen, feeling increasingly dizzy.

I had come to the conclusion that the best course of action would be to curl up in a corner and cry until Joe got home, when Hallie walked in behind me. "Oh, my . . ."

The neighbor girls appeared from downstairs, followed by Donnell and Lane.

"Is that what I think it is?"

"Oh, disgusting!"

"The smell!"

I silenced the voices behind me and told them in shaky words that they could return downstairs. Hallie left with them but returned quickly with a dark-colored towel. "Wrap her in this to pick her up," she said in the tone of a military general announcing the battle plan. "I'll start the bath. You bring her right in."

I did as I was told. Hallie left the bathroom just as I entered, and she returned with a trash bag. With the water filling the tub behind me, I peeled off Lucy's shirt and socks, dropping each item directly into the bag while Hallie held it.

"Do you want to try to wash these?" she asked.

The look I gave her didn't require words. These clothes could have been hand-made and smuggled out of a war zone by my great-great-grandmother and my first choice would still have been to incinerate them. I tossed the towel in the bag too, and Hallie disappeared to throw it all away. I plopped Lucy in the bath. As I slowly and pitifully went to work on her hair, I reminded myself to put *hazmat suit* at the top of my Christmas list this year.

It took the better part of an hour to get her clean, and all the while I tried not to think of adjectives to describe the texture of the bath water. I had to drain the tub, refill it, drain it again, and then clean it with bleach before the final wash. When I considered the disaster that awaited me in her room—the sheets, the toys, the caked stuffed animal fur, the carpet—I imagined politely asking everyone to please step outside and then burning down the house.

When the bath was finished Lucy went happily on her way, doing her backward army crawl down the stairs to play with her siblings. I prepared myself to face my fate. I pulled my hair into a pony tail and sucked in a breath. I was honestly worried about vomiting when I saw the mess, so when I stepped into the room I closed my eyes. Then I opened them.

It was clean.

The whole room was clean. There were even fresh sheets on the crib. It was as if the whole thing had never happened, and it was all just the scatological nightmare of a deeply disturbed mind. I started shouting again, equally incoherent, but this time using a different choice of words.

"I hope you don't mind. I rinsed the sheets with the outside hose before I put them in the washer," Hallie called from the playroom, where she was currently organizing the toys. "I put the water on extra hot."

I stumbled over to her. "You . . . cleaned all of that?"

"The stuffed animals took a little work, but I think they're good now. I set them on the back porch to dry. The toys are in bleach in the kitchen sink."

My mind raced to come up with some way to express to her what this meant to me. Maybe I could offer free babysitting services for life? Serenade her with an a cappella version of "Wind Beneath My Wings"? Get a mural tattooed on my back that depicted her riding a unicorn? Stand outside her window with a huge boom box like the guy in *Say Anything*? I was open to any and all ideas.

After the house settled down again, I finally cleared my mind enough to get to work on the book. As I started, a new emotion descended upon me: sheer, utter mortification. This is exactly why I didn't want anyone's assistance! Whenever I turned down offers of help I always justified it by thinking, *I don't want anyone else to see my mess*. Little did I know how valid that fear was!

In the middle of elaborate planning to adopt a new identity and start our family's lives over in another country, a thought came to mind: *Maybe this is what an answered prayer looks like.*

I had been complaining for weeks that I was struggling with everything I had on my plate, all the while turning down offers of help. Hallie had made this offer many times before, and I said no. The neighbor girls always said they'd be happy to watch the big kids if I wanted to sneak into my office, and I always demurred. I'd recently run into a woman at church who'd stumbled across my blog, was excited to read that I was writing a book, and offered to have a takeout dinner brought to our family to free up my time one evening. I responded with my mantra: "No, I couldn't possibly."

I'd often wondered how my blogger friend, Ann, and others like her could balance things so well. Sometimes it seemed like they were secretly given an extra twelve hours in each day or magic powers that the rest of us were denied. But now I considered that maybe people like Ann were just more open to God moving in their lives in ways that took them outside of their comfort zones.

19

If You're Happy and You Know It

MANY MONTHS LATER, the manuscript for the book was almost finished. It had taken me so, so much longer than I'd expected: Baby Kate was now over a year old. I'd first started working with Ted almost two years before. My progress had been hampered by a never-ending stream of interruptions that would have made the creativity gurus take me by the hand and say, "Maybe it's time to give up."

But I was almost done, and I felt a rush of electric anticipation about moving on to the next step—and maybe even finding a publisher. I had a lot of strikes against me—unpublished author, not well known, no experience in the industry—but Ted was a highly respected agent, and there was a real possibility he could open doors for me. Even if I got only rejections, at least we'd know.

I had no illusions that I would become the next Dean Koontz, but there was a real possibility that I could at least bring in enough income from this project that it could relieve some of our financial pressure. Not only did we need a bigger house, but the old minivan we'd purchased when Lucy was born was now falling apart. The big problem was that the driver's side door broke; there was no way to open it. At six feet tall, with all of my height in my legs, it was an arduous process to scoot past the center console to exit the passenger side door (and I had a bulging, purple bruise on my knee to prove it). So I'd started going through the window. On a recent evening a neighbor actually stopped walking his dog and stared for the entire procedure of me climbing out of my minivan. It was not the fluid, *Dukes-of-Hazzard* maneuver I'd imagined it to be, and in fact ended with me landing on one foot and hopping forward before I stumbled into the grass. The neighbor shook his head and resumed walking his dog.

So we needed money for car repairs, in addition to a bigger house. It was time to get this book finished. I let the kids watch egregious amounts of television and would return to them after a writing session with the guilty demeanor of a dog who'd chewed up a dress shoe. I got up too early. I stayed up too late.

Yet, whenever I was writing, it didn't feel like work. A concerned commenter on my blog asked why I would want to undertake this project when I had my hands so full at home; the answer was that it was *because* I was so maxed out in my daily life that I needed this outlet. The process of writing didn't sap my energy; as is always the case with blue flames, this work *gave* me energy when I did it. I'd begun to hear other people talk about this phenomenon as well (not in person, since I had basically no social life, but I'd heard about it on the internet). One blogger absolutely loved knitting, another delighted in cooking, and yet another was into music. Another woman I followed had created a garden that was so vast and over-flowing that it was as if she had a small farm in her backyard.

All of our gifts were different: the gardener woman probably thought that hours of writing sounded like torture, and I had already decided that if the world food supply collapsed I was just going to have to be one of the people who starved to death. But all of us agreed on one thing: this work did not drain us but in fact filled us up.

On a Tuesday morning, I clicked through a list of edits I'd made during my read-through, deleting a paragraph here, rewording a sentence there. I couldn't help but grin as I watched this project come together. I was proud of it. I'd worked hard, and I felt confident that I'd told this story to the best of my ability. I finished a page of edits and flipped to the next page. Which was blank. There were no more edits. I was done.

I wanted Hallie to read it and give me feedback, so I printed a copy and even picked up a decorative binder during a grocery trip. It had a mint-colored background with a delicate floral pattern printed in white, which added a touch of class to my work. I painstakingly three-hole punched the pages in thin stacks, assembled them in the pretty binder, and even included a cover page as if I were trying to impress my high school English teacher.

At the end of the week, I packed up the kids to go to Hallie's house for a playdate and manuscript delivery trip. On the way over, I heard what sounded like water splashing in the back of the car. I thought my ears must be deceiving me since we didn't bring any drinks.

Donnell enlightened me. "Lucy threw up!"

"I throw up too!" Lane said from her seat next to Lucy. Another stomach flu had been going around the area, and evidently it had just reached the Fulwiler minivan.

I pulled up in front of Hallie's house and squeezed myself into the back of the vehicle, using an old roll of paper towels to get things cleaned up until we could get back home. Needless to say, there would be no playdate. I got back behind the wheel so I could get these plague-ridden kids to the house, where they could vomit all over the couch instead of the car. Just as the wheels rolled forward, I remembered the book. I rolled down the passenger window and tossed the decorative binder out onto the sidewalk. I'd aimed for a nice landing, but instead it splattered open, the pages fanning unevenly where the jaws of the binder coil had snapped. I called Hallie and told her that we were turning around and that she would find my beloved project scattered all over her sidewalk.

Hallie loved the manuscript, and we both pretended to believe her many assertions that she was not at all biased by our friendship.

After a quick read-through by Joe, I sent it to Ted. It was such an enormous moment that I took a picture of the email with the attachment and posted it on my blog.

While I waited for his response, I watched Ted's Twitter posts obsessively, assuming that every update was a secret commentary on my project. One day passed, then two, then three. I could hardly contain my nervousness and excitement. He would probably want a few revisions, and then we'd begin the work of finding a publisher. I became giddy whenever I dared to imagine what the next few weeks would look like.

When his response finally arrived, I was standing in the living room, eating handfuls of sea salt and vinegar chips straight from the bag while the kids watched Barney. My laptop sat on its usual spot on top of the fireplace, and the new, bolded item in my inbox caught my attention. I threw the chips in the general direction of the table and ran to the screen. Ted said he wanted me to call him.

A cold sweat spread over my skin. I noticed that he didn't say he loved it. His tone did not seem to indicate that this call was necessary because there were too many good things to fit into one email. "It's ready to go!" is not a statement that requires verbal communication.

I fished my cell phone from my jeans pocket and dialed his number. I knew I was playing with fire by trying to do this now. Casual phone calls had ceased to be part of my normal life around the time Lucy was born. My conversations always got interrupted so that I ended up speaking sentences like, "I'd like to speak with customer service about *what is on your face?*" But, for the moment, the kids were zoned out to Barney. Maybe this could work.

I started the call with nervous chatter, then finally shut up and let Ted speak. He listed what he liked about the pages he'd read, and my sense of foreboding increased with every compliment. When he finished his summary of all the good stuff, he paused.

"There's a 'but,' isn't there?" I asked.

"THERE'S A BUTT!" Donnell shouted from the couch, sending his sisters into fits of giggles.

"Yes. There is," Ted said gravely.

I would have replied that "it sounds like there's a big 'but,'" but I was afraid the kids might explode with ecstasy.

"It needs work."

I noticed he didn't say "some" work or "just a little teeny, tiny, itty, bitty bit" of work. Lane complained that she couldn't hear the TV and turned up the volume about twenty clicks. Barney was talking about words that describe your feelings. I noticed that *fatalistic despair* wasn't on the list.

"How much work?"

"A lot."

Ted began to lay out the problems with the manuscript, and they were huge. Worse, he was right. Now that I saw the draft through his eyes, the flaws were so clear. I stepped backward into the kitchen to put distance between myself and the loud, purple dinosaur who was clapping and jumping with carefree elation. "The changes that we're talking about here don't seem to be within the scope of a standard revision," I said.

Ted agreed.

"I mean . . ." the words caught in my throat. I couldn't bring myself to say them. Barney's band started up, and the kids turned the volume louder. I was so disconnected from reality that I barely registered the noise or any awareness that I could do something about it, as if I were having this call in the middle of a thunderstorm. I raised my voice so he could hear me. "It sounds like we're talking about a rewrite. Like, starting this whole thing from scratch."

"You're probably looking at something like that."

I ended the call as politely and professionally as possible, then stumbled back into a kitchen chair. I stared ahead, frozen like a statue of a failed writer. In the background, Barney started singing *"If You're Happy and You Know It."*

"Mommy, clap yo hands!" Lucy called from the living room. With all of my career dreams crashing down around me, I forced a smile for her. And when Barney and his dinosaur friends sung, *If you're happy and you know it, clap your hands!* I *clap-clapped*, right on cue.

20

Bible Charades

IF I WORRIED THAT I WAS NOT A REAL WRITER after such a spectacular failure with the manuscript, I should have taken comfort in the fact that I could do writer drama with the best of them. I moped. I sighed dramatically when anything about the book came up. I listlessly pushed a plate of lasagna away at the dinner table (then I caught a whiff of the meat sauce and had three helpings).

Joe kept telling me to shake off the setback and get back to work. On the way to church the Sunday morning after the rejection, he said, "You're going to let one person's feedback bother you this much?"

"Yes." I turned the radio on the back speakers so the kids wouldn't be exposed to their mother's hyperbolic pessimism (and wondered when minivan makers will finally start including a soundproof, roll-up limousine window as a standard feature). "It's more than one person's opinion. It's a top literary agent pointing out that the manuscript that I poured almost two years of my life into is an irretrievable disaster."

Joe frowned at the road in front of him. "Everyone has to work at their craft. Everyone—even people with God-given gifts. Michelangelo spent his entire young life studying under masters of the arts. You think you're better than Michelangelo that you can jump into the work you love and nail it on your first try?"

He had a good point. I ignored it so I could keep the tortured artist vibe going. "Here's the other thing," I said. "I don't have peace about jumping into a brand new draft of the book."

This whole endeavor of trying to launch a writing career hadn't turned out the way I thought it would. Back when I said yes to Ted, on that summer day when Joe and I were standing in our front yard, I had this lofty idea about how the creation of a family and the creation of meaningful work were both ways of encountering God. I thought it would be a gift to myself and to my family to ignite my blue flame—and, eventually, hopefully, bring in a little income from it. "But now I see that I was wrong and I have no talent and I've wasted everyone's time."

Joe shook his head in lieu of responding to my drama. "So what's your plan now?" he asked.

"Maybe I should look more seriously at going back to tech work. Or I could not work at all. It puts more pressure on you in terms of finances, but maybe it'd be better if I had more time for household stuff."

"I don't think you should give up on this dream," Joe said.

"I don't have peace with going back to writing right now."

"Do you have peace with walking away from it?"

A full mile of highway passed before I responded. "No."

After Mass, a woman stood up in front of the congregation and announced an upcoming women's retreat. She shared a moving testimonial about how her life had been transformed by it. She wasn't even finished with her speech before I elbowed Joe and whispered that I wanted to go. I hadn't been very involved in our church community because I was so maxed out at home, so this seemed like a perfect opportunity to rekindle my prayer life—and maybe even meet some other women. I imagined spending all morning praying and reading Scripture, then having quiet conversations with fellow retreatants over meals.

Two weeks later, I was waking up on a church bus as it pulled up to the retreat center, which was located in a rural area an hour outside of town. After I shook myself awake and gathered my backpack, I stepped out onto the gravel drive to find myself at an unmarked building. Farm land stretched to the horizon; the only sign of civilization was a dilapidated hayloft about a mile away. I felt disoriented, like the people in the TV shows who have been kidnapped and taken to the terrorists' bunker.

The building contained a lofty auditorium space, which was flanked by a chapel, two sleeping quarters packed with bunk beds, and an industrial kitchen. The structure rumbled with thunderous sounds of commotion from inside. When the retreat leaders opened the doors, it was an explosion of light and sound. There was music. There were shouts of welcome. There were hand-decorated signs with glitter and streamers. The organizers all wore bright pink t-shirts, whose vibrant hue matched their cheerful personalities. Women hopped off the bus behind me, rushing up to other women with hugs and squealed exclamations of greeting, giving the impression that pretty much everyone but me had come with a friend.

In my rush to get away, I had not looked into the details of this weekend before I signed up. And that, it now occurred to me, was a grave error.

In my defense, I had no idea that Catholics even did retreats like this. I had many Evangelical friends (again, "friends" meaning "people I talked to on my computer from the shadowy recesses of my home") who described events at their churches as riotously fun gatherings where people sung and waved their hands and used the word *fellowship* as a verb. I had counted on my Catholic brethren to put together an emotionless, entirely cerebral retreat, and now it seemed that they had failed me completely.

A woman ran up to greet me. "JENNIFER! Welcome, sister!" I forgot that I'd been handed a nametag back in the parking lot where we met the bus, and in my sleepy state I was dazzled by her supernatural knowledge of my name. I was snapped awake, however, when she slipped my cell phone from my hand and dropped it into the wicker basket she held at her side. "I'll take that, honey. Have an amazing weekend!" I turned to follow her, wondering if she was one of those pickpockets you see on the news who's so confident that nobody ever reports them. Then I noticed other women gladly handing over their devices. Evidently this was part of the retreat.

With Joe and four little kids at home, the idea of not having access to my phone for the entire weekend made me feel shaky. I was about to chase down the woman who took it when another lady intercepted me and announced that we were about to start praise and worship. I didn't know if she was an organizer or another hostage or what, but I asked, "Do you have a copy of the schedule I can look at?"

She beamed with excitement. "They don't give us schedules. It's all a surprise!"

I stood in the entry way of the retreat center, the sensory jumble of bright colors and happy sounds swirling all around me, the realization descending upon me with great force and speed that this wasn't the silent retreat I'd expected it to be. For an introvert who lived in a house with constant noise and unexpected interruptions, who desperately needed some quiet time to think and reflect, this was my personal version of Dante's *Inferno*.

There was singing mixed with hand-holding; lively chatter in the dormitory late into the night; group leaders waking us at dawn with loud, gleeful songs of praise. At one point I was gently and lovingly dragged from the chapel where I'd been praying because it was time to participate in a dance competition set to Christian music.

Even in the midst of it, I could see the goodness of the people there. The women who organized it did the entire thing on a volunteer basis, and they poured their souls into the event. The other attendees were friendly, open, and genuinely wanted to become better people through the weekend. If I weren't in a season of life when I was constantly overstimulated to begin with, even I might have enjoyed it.

As it was, when the final event of the final evening rolled around, I was a basket case. I had never had a true panic attack in my life, but I was pretty sure it was about to happen here. The combination of feeling mentally at my limit with not having a phone or a car made me feel raw and powerless in a way I had only rarely experienced before.

Luckily, this final activity was what I'd been yearning for when I signed up for this retreat. A half dozen priests from across the diocese were coming in, and each would be available for confession and spiritual counseling. As we gathered in the main hall beforehand, one of the organizers hushed the crowd for an announcement.

"I'm afraid we have some bad news," she said. "Father George, whom many of you know, has had a tragedy happen in his family." She explained that, just an hour before, Fr. George had received the news that both his niece and his nephew had been killed in a car accident. He would, of course, need to leave for the airport to be with his family, and now we'd be short a priest.

We milled into lines accordingly, all of us stunned as we processed the news. Though I did not know this Fr. George, many of the women there did, and they were openly stricken on his behalf. The room took on a somber, prayerful tone. For the first time since we arrived, there was silence.

Makeshift confessionals were set up throughout the building: one behind a screen on the stage at the front of the room, another just inside the kitchen. I got in line for one in which the priest was stationed at the end of a long hall, mainly because it had the shortest line.

When I took my seat, I was met with the kindly face of a man who appeared to be in his fifties. He put me at ease immediately. I couldn't place this priest's accent, but he reminded me of our friends from Mumbai, so I guessed he was from India. I made my confession, and then, afterwards, he asked what else was on my mind.

"This is going to sound silly," I said. "But I'm struggling to figure out whether or not I should do some work that I love."

I told him everything. I was one of the last people in the line, and there was still plenty of time, so I went into detail about my situation. I told him about the call I'd felt to have a big family, despite the fact that I'd give myself a C-minus in parenting most days. I told him about how I yearned to build a writing career for my own fulfillment and also to help pay the bills. I told him about the rejection and how I'd have to start again at square one if this book were ever to be written. For the first time since I'd arrived, my body relaxed, the stress pouring out of me like a lance draining a wound.

When I finished, he was quiet for a long moment. He rested his head on his clasped hands, as if he were thinking or praying or both.

Finally, he spoke. "Congratulations," he said.

"I'm sorry?"

"Congratulations! You said you're writing a book."

"Oh, yes. Okay. Thanks!"

"This must be exciting for your family."

"I guess so. But that's the thing: I worry that it's not a good thing for the kids."

"But have you brought them into it?"

"In what way?" I tried to imagine what that would look like, but my mind stalled out with a vision of the last time I tried to write in the living room, when Lane and Lucy took turns climbing on my head.

"Are you thinking of all of this, this book and the other things you do, are you thinking of it in terms of your family or in terms of yourself?"

"I'm not sure I follow . . ."

"Remember this," he said. "Where there is no unity, there is no God. God is always calling us to connection, to unity, and if we don't have that, we are not walking with God." As he spoke, his face radiated joy as if a light had been switched on inside of him. He was one of those people who's filled with an undefinable yet palpably present grace that makes you feel warm and safe.

Yet I wasn't sure what his words, as wise as they were, had to do with my conundrum. Luckily, he elaborated.

"Do this work that God is calling you to do, but do it as one part of something bigger—your family." His eyes shone with genuine concern. "Have you ever asked what work your family is supposed to do together?"

"Well . . . no. I haven't."

"We always think like individuals, like the work that we do has nothing to do with anyone else. God wants us to see what we do as just one small part of something greater . . ."

"Like a symphony." I didn't mean to interrupt, but I finally understood what he was getting at, and the words escaped from my lips without me even realizing it. I imagined an orchestra belting out a Beethoven piece: each member plays her own tune but does it with the goal of creating something greater, with others.

"Yes! Like that. Unite with your family. Bring them into what you do, and bring what you do into your family. Move in unity, not apart from one another." My mind was on high alert so that I could absorb every word he said. "My child, if you do this, you will find joy—more joy than you can imagine. Don't forget that."

It was time for me to go, so he gave me a final blessing. Time seemed to stop as he whispered the words of prayer over me, and for that infinite moment, I felt nothing but peace.

When I got back into the auditorium, I realized I never did catch his name. I looked over my shoulder at the handwritten note taped on a wall near the hallway, which said:

Fr. George

I pulled one of the organizers aside and asked if this was a different priest with the same name. She shook her head.

"No, this is the Fr. George we mentioned earlier. His flight is later in the evening, so he came up here before he has to leave. Isn't he just darling?"

I looked back toward the hallway, trying to process the fact that I had been speaking with the same priest who'd just found out that he lost multiple beloved family members. The organizer went on to tell me that he was from Pakistan and grew up in extreme poverty in a remote village where he was persecuted for his faith. I thanked her and wandered into the chapel, where I settled into a pew at the back.

The door had been left open, and I heard a crescendo of voices just outside. I twisted around to see that Fr. George was leaving, and a group of women and other clergy had gathered around him to console him. And yet, to look only at body language, it appeared that he was consoling them. He moved easily and peacefully as he shook another priest's hand; his gaze was steady and welcoming when a woman grabbed him by the hand spoke to him.

I'd been reading the work of Thomas Merton, a world-traveling agnostic who left everything to become a monk. One of his lines I'd highlighted came to mind now: "Love is our true destiny. We do not find the meaning of life by ourselves alone—we find it with another. We do not discover the secret of our lives merely by study and calculation in our own isolated meditations. The meaning of our life is a secret that has to be revealed to us in love."

A wave of tears overflowed from deep within me, and I didn't even try to stop it. I simply sat, closed my eyes, and let myself sit with the gratitude and relief and exhaustion I felt in this moment.

A warm hand touched mine, and one of the retreat leaders appeared at my side. She eased herself into the pew next to me and lovingly placed her arm around my shoulders. Then she leaned in close and whispered, "Jennifer, it's time to play Bible Charades."

21

Tex-Mex Epiphany

I ONCE SAW A PRODUCT ON AMAZON CALLED THE RELAXMAN. It's a white sleep capsule with vague resemblance to a space ship in which you can enclose yourself to shut out the world completely, available for the bargain price of $85,995 (plus $2,500 shipping). All throughout the extrovert retreat I fantasized about having one of these fine items. I imagined waving at my fellow retreatants and shouting "Y'all have fun!" over their singing before I pressed the button to close the lid on my hermetically sealed tube. I figured that in order to recover I would have to create a poor man's version of this product by wrapping myself in blankets, sliding on my largest headphones, and zoning out to TV or a book after the kids went to bed.

Yet after my conversation with Fr. George, I was filled with a new energy that stayed with me through the rest of the retreat. When I got home, I charged into the house, scooping up the kids for hugs and kisses, and told Joe that I couldn't wait to talk. I felt like I'd been carrying around a wrapped gift—one that I could now tear open and unpack with him.

That night, after the kids were asleep, we set wine glasses on the table between us, the logos of the wineries where we bought them almost entirely scrubbed away by too many runs through the dishwasher (hand washing wine glasses stopped being a thing in our house around child number two). I told Joe everything the kindly priest had said to me. As we contrasted Fr. George's advice to our current approach to work and life, we realized his suggestion wasn't just a minor tweak to the way we were doing things; it would involve a fundamental shift.

Fr. George's words were the fruit of an entirely different world-view from that of the modern United States. Recalling that he was from Pakistan, I thought of the Pakistani babysitter who worked for us when Donnell was a baby. I remembered being confused by the choices that she and folks in her circles made: She mentioned a cousin who passed up a prestigious job opportunity to stay close to his elderly parents. She got her extended family's input on a big school decision she had to make. Because I'd always been steeped in a worldview in which personal autonomy is seen as the primary path to happiness, these kinds of decisions struck me as a recipe for dissatisfaction. What if she didn't like her family's input? What if her cousin never got another cool job opportunity? It now dawned on me that these choices were borne out of an entirely different set of convictions about what really leads to fulfillment in life.

Joe pointed out that many of our friends from other countries and cultures saw interdependence on family as a natural part of life. Just the week before, a family friend had taken off days of much-needed work to help an ailing brother back in Mexico. It never occurred to her not to go to him, even though taking the time off meant she would now struggle to pay her bills. Other family members came together to help her help him, pooling their funds to assist her in covering rent that month. The way they saw it, you make time for your work as it fits into your family; you don't make time for family as it fits into your work.

Until this conversation, I had never realized just how different my own view was. Now, I thought for the first time, "What if there's another way to see this?"

As a result of that conversation, we decided to come up with a family vision. Joe and I had spent most of our adult lives laying out detailed plans for personal achievements; now, we realized that we had never done the same for our family. To borrow from the analogy in the conversation with Fr. George, we'd been planning our lives as if we were a group of soloists, all of us playing our own tunes on the same stage. Now, we wanted to see what kind of symphony we could create if we started thinking like an orchestra.

My mom volunteered to babysit that Saturday night so we could go out to dinner, and we headed to our favorite Tex-Mex spot, located in a shopping center that was nestled into a wide network of neighborhoods near our house. We settled into a table on the outdoor patio, the chips and salsa arriving before we finished scooting in our chairs. Under the protective spread of an old cedar elm, with the precise, colorful notes of a Spanish guitar album in the background, we set out to dream about what our ideal version of family life would look like. We laid a notebook open on the table that we'd pulled from the kids' art supplies just before we left the house.

"What are three words that would describe our ideal family culture?" Joe asked. He wrote the same question at the top of the page.

After a discussion so lively that the waiter approached but walked away twice, we came up with *creative, entrepreneurial,* and *Christian.* It wasn't a perfect list, and we knew that we'd probably end up tweaking these adjectives or even replacing them altogether. But even having this rudimentary set of words to key off of instantly shifted the way I thought about our family's life. We started a new page, and I wrote the three words in all caps at the center. I slid the notebook back in between the two of us, and we asked ourselves, *If someone were to observe our family for a day, would they come up with these words?*

It had been a particularly rough afternoon, with none of the kids sleeping well the night before and a variety of messy disasters occurring, so I noted that this was a bad time to ask that question. If someone had seen our house today they would have handed back a list that said *warlike, loud,* and *sticky.* Nonetheless, it was a fascinating exercise to take a look at how we conducted ourselves on a daily basis and see how well we were actually putting these ideals into practice.

The discussion also left me feeling lightened by a new and unexpected sense of freedom. As Joe and I talked about the *entrepreneurial* adjective, we discussed how we were the kind of family that enjoyed testing out new technology. Thanks to our tech backgrounds, he and I were early adopters of things like e-readers, social media, blogging, and smart home devices. We'd begun looking into how apps might help us with education, and Donnell was already talking about learning to write code. When I articulated this facet of our family's collective personality, I could accept certain areas in which we might have different standards than other people; for example, we would always do more screen time than families who weren't as into technology as we were. I also started to let go of my obsession with other lifestyles that were alluring for various reasons but weren't ultimately a good fit for us.

Just that morning I'd read a blog post by a mom who described her family's lifestyle as "intellectual crunchy." They lived on ten acres of land with a sprawling garden that was managed entirely by the kids, who spent most of their days outdoors. They even had a goat, whose milk they used to make cheese and hand-crafted cakes of soap. Each night, one of the parents read aloud from a classic work of literature while the kids washed vegetables from the garden. When I saw this over my morning cup of coffee, I was rocked by the usual wave of insecurity-panic that made me want to spit out my drink, throw our TV into the Goodwill dumpster, and return to the house with a goat under one arm and a volume of Virgil's major works under the other. But now I was taking the first steps toward a place where I could appreciate other families' ways of doing things without falling into guilt or comparison.

With a plate of steak nachos in front of us and an easy breeze that hinted at the cooler fall weather to come, we filled up six more pages of notes and ideas. We asked questions like *What would our perfect day look like?* and *How can we have a cohesive family culture where individual talents shine as well?* and covered pages with our answers. But the biggest revelation came at the very end of the discussion.

Joe suggested that we do an inventory of our challenges and our blessings. We didn't have much of an extended family support network, with Joe, me, and my dad being only children, Yaya being estranged from much of her family, and my mom's siblings living thousands of miles away. However, we had a tremendous resource in our parents. My mom was only a couple of miles away; Yaya visited often and had been talking about moving nearby if we were going to stay here over the long term. My dad mentioned that he planned to retire in this area as well. And Papaw lived just ten miles up the road, which allowed our kids to have a close connection with their great-grandfather.

We both shook our heads in awed gratitude. "We're so lucky to have all of this," Joe said. "We'd be crazy to throw it away."

I knew exactly what he meant. Earlier in the conversation, we'd once again touched on the subject of moving. As part of Joe's continuing research on this subject, he'd identified a part of the state we could relocate to where housing prices were cheaper, and his income would be higher for the same amount of work. Moving there would instantly resolve most of the financial crunch we were feeling.

And now, once and for all, we took that option off the table.

We talked about how that same opportunity could be the perfect answer for a different family. Hallie and Dan had recently asked similar questions, and they'd decided that the best path for them was going to involve moving out of Austin, then probably moving again after that. I smiled when I thought of Joe's friend from law school who ended up buying an RV and traveling full-time with his wife and their three young children. Each of these families had an entirely different set of advantages and disadvantages to work with and had crafted lifestyles that smoothed over their challenges and maximized their blessings. Now, finally, we were doing the same.

We agreed that we wouldn't speak of moving anymore. This created new pressures: Joe estimated that we could scrape by another year on just his income, but that was about it. In twelve to eighteen months, something would have to give. But we would think about all of that later.

When we left the restaurant, I paused at the gate of the patio to take in the moment. A slight chill had swept into the night air, and it seemed to hint at fresh starts. This vision we were concocting for our family was still vague, but I had no question that we were on the right path now. I jogged to catch up with Joe, the notebook clutched to my side, filled with that same mix of feeling daunted and excited as when you're at the top of a big hill on a roller coaster and you're just about to go over the other side.

22

Banana Man

I HAD NOT YET STARTED REWRITING THE BOOK, though this time it wasn't because I was being a drama queen. I wanted to continue fleshing out these new ideas about work and family life, and Donnell was starting school. I was okay with hitting the pause button on my own work, even though money worries always lingered in the back of my mind. In the symphony that we were starting to play, it was my turn to put down my instrument.

Donnell was attending kindergarten at a local public charter school. I was climbing the learning curve of being a school mom, absorbing valuable lessons like the importance of being the first to make a food commitment for class potluck parties. As soon as I saw a sign-up list, I'd elbow aside other parents to get my name next to an item, because the lists all looked something like this:

- 2 bags of baby carrots
- 3 loaves of bread
- 3 bags of potato chips
- 1 bunch of green grapes
- 1 dozen gluten-free, sugar-free, dairy-free cupcakes, each decorated to represent a different character from *Moby Dick*

And if you're the last one to sign up, you know which one you're going to get.

Meanwhile, Lane and Lucy were attending the church Mother's Day Out program two mornings per week. With all the school drop-offs and pickups, I was starting to consider the car my second home.

Halloween fell on a Sunday, and I noticed that morning at church that I felt a pinching in my right leg whenever I stood. This was the leg that had the blood clot when I was pregnant with Lane, and it had sustained permanent damage. That ankle was purple with a spray of broken blood vessels, and that calf was an inch wider in circumference than the other one, bulging with varicose veins. Normally, the leg didn't bother me aside from how it looked. However, in early pregnancy I always felt a pain in the spot where I'd had the clot. It went away as soon as I began doing the blood-thinner shots, but it was one of the reasons I'd suspected I was pregnant the last two times around.

And now the pain was back.

My first chance to take a test came after Joe got home and my mom arrived to help the kids get into their costumes. I grabbed cans of glitter hair spray and pastel face paint to turn Lane and Lucy into princesses, and Donnell pulled on his skeleton costume. Kate was being helped into her tiger outfit by my mom. When everyone was set, I excused myself to go put on my own costume and snuck upstairs to take a test.

Immediately, there were two lines. Baby number five was on the way. When he or she was born, we'd have five kids under age seven. It didn't seem like the perfect time for a baby to come along, but it never did. I always felt like we could have a little more money, more space in the house, or more things accomplished without the demands of a newborn. I was starting to recognize that it always feels problematic to fit another child into your family when you're contemplating pregnancy. Yet when that child arrives, his or her life is instantly intertwined with yours in a way that feels so right that it's as if there were never a possibility of this person not existing. The minute you see that baby, the whole universe retroactively adjusts itself so that this life was meant to exist all along.

My mom called to me from downstairs, so I tossed the test in the trash. I grabbed a keyboard to complete my costume ("Writer," which was not going to win me any creativity awards) and hurried to rejoin the group. My dad had just arrived to take pictures, and Joe was putting the finishing touches on his own outfit.

A year before, Joe and I had been surfing the web together, a laptop sitting half on my lap, half on his, when we stumbled across a picture of a man wearing a banana costume. I laughed and was about to click away, but Joe stopped me. He was captivated by this masterpiece and announced that he must own it.

"Halloween's a long way away," I said at the time.

"What does that have to do with anything?"

"It's a costume. Where else would you wear it?"

Joe pitied my lack of vision. He proclaimed that the correct question for this outfit was not "Where would you wear it?" but rather "Where *wouldn't* you wear it?"

I surprised him with it as a Christmas present, and he was more excited than the kids were when Santa brought them a rocking horse. When we were first dating, I'd noticed how proud Joe was of his custom tuxedo, which he'd special ordered from an exclusive tailor in Hong Kong when he graduated from business school. He bemoaned the fact that there weren't more opportunities naturally suited for such a magnificent outfit, and he promised to don it as often as possible, even if it made people uncomfortable. Now he spoke the same way about the banana suit.

Our crew headed out for trick-or-treating, the gentleman banana leading the way, with two princesses, a skeleton, a tiger, and a writer trailing behind. My mom picked up Kate, the confused tiger, while directing the skeleton, and my dad held the two princesses' hands. I pulled Joe back so we could talk.

"Remember when I told you a few days ago I thought I might be pregnant?"

Joe stopped and turned to me. "Oh my gosh. Are you?"

"Yup."

He reached out to hug me, but I couldn't quite get my arms

around the unwieldy costume so we ended up patting each other on the hands. I put my finger to my lips to signal that I didn't want others to hear just yet.

"So how do you feel about this?" I asked.

"I want to wait until I know how you feel. I'll be devastated or excited or whatever you want me to be."

I laughed. "I'm really okay with it. I'm kind of starting to see that it never feels like a perfect time to have another kid, you know?"

We watched our little crew run up to the door of a neighbor's house. Lucy shouted, "Gimme candy!" and we could hear Donnell's murmured voice correcting her Halloween etiquette.

Joe was lost in thought. "Wow. That's a lot of little kids in one house." We walked for a few more moments in silence. Now that Kate, who was one and a half, had had her first experience of getting chocolates and lollipops dumped into a bag by strangers, she got the concept and got it well. She shoved her siblings and grandparents aside as she toddled determinedly to the next house, holding her bag out in front of her in case any passersby wanted to throw in more goodies as well.

As we rounded a corner, Joe seemed to have come to a big conclusion that he wanted to announce. I assumed that he was going to share a new strategy for how we could further tighten our budget. Instead, he said, "It's time to hire a babysitter."

"What? What are you talking about?" Of all the things I thought he might suggest that we needed to do in response to this news, that was pretty much the last thing I would have guessed. "With what money?"

"We have that money we put away toward a better minivan. We can use that."

I stopped. "Joe. This is crazy talk. We have to have a new car."

"Our car works. It gets us from place to place." We'd managed to get the driver's side door fixed, which undoubtedly disappointed the neighbors who were enjoying the free entertainment of me climbing in and out of the window, but it still had a whole host of other problems.

"Hey, banana!" A neighborhood dad yelled from across the street. Joe held up his fist in a man-to-man gesture of camaraderie and strength.

"Also, this current minivan will be totally maxed out when this baby gets here," I pointed out. "It only seats seven. We'd barely have room for groceries or luggage or anything else."

We resumed walking to follow my parents and the kids. "Look. Yes. I agree that if we could go shake a money tree in the backyard and then buy whatever we wanted, we should get a newer car *and* a bigger house *and* a babysitter and maybe an extra banana suit as well. But we can't. And so we have to prioritize. And I really think that getting help for you is more important than those other things."

Joe had an expression for situations like this, and it was one of my favorites: *Life isn't about having it all, but about being good at not having it all.* I tended to drift from one want or need to another, without pausing to ask if there was actually something we wanted or needed even more that would be a better use of our limited resources. Joe's business school background had trained him to prioritize ruthlessly, even when it meant making unexpected choices. Like this one.

"I'm not saying a car or house upgrade isn't important. I think those things are really important, actually. I'm just saying that you having some help with the kids is more important."

I was appreciative but a little perplexed. "So I get to stay home with the kids and not bring in an income and still have household help? I thought only the women from *Real Housewives* did that."

I had justified the temporary hire of Terri and a couple of other sitters over the years because I was at least attempting to make money at those times. I still planned to get back to work with writing, but my expectations about income were much humbler this time around. Therefore, I had assumed that childcare help would not be part of my life anytime soon.

"Think about what Yaya and Papaw were saying when Lucy was a baby, about how unnatural your life is in modern suburbia," Joe said. "Never in human history have parents raised kids in isolation. Never. People always had their clans or villages or tribes or whatever to help them. Kids ran around with other kids. People lived in multigenerational houses where grandmothers or nieces or cousins would be around to hold a baby or help cook. Or, like Papaw and Yaya, they roamed around their farmland all day."

"When my mom was a kid, she and her siblings and friends ran around for hours without their parents even knowing where they were," I said, starting to see where Joe was going with this.

"Heeeeeeey banana man!"

"Banaaaannnnna!"

Joe did his solidarity fist to more men walking in the mellow sunset light with their mermaids and wizards, then he turned back to me.

"Before the modern age, you simply don't see people even trying to raise children all on their own—you see them sharing the work with their villages."

"And so hiring a babysitter replaces the village?"

"Exactly. People didn't used to have grocery bills because there were animals around to hunt. Grocery expenses are a natural part of modern life to compensate for the fact that we can't walk outside and spear the nearest animal for dinner."

"The neighbors might not appreciate that."

"And that's how I've come to think of childcare. It's an expense like groceries—people didn't used to need to spend that money, but now they do. It's something that's worth trying really hard to fit into the budget, if there's any way you can, because it's something you were designed to need but you don't have in your natural environment."

It occurred to me that there were other ways to ease stay-at-home parents' burdens as well. I'd seen people move out to land, where their children could safely escape the confines of the house for hours at a time. Here in suburban Texas, families often bought spacious homes where the kids could wander between multiple playrooms to keep themselves amused without their moms playing entertainment director. And all of the options achieved the same effect: relieving at-home parents from the pressures that come from the highly unnatural situation of having their children all up in their faces all day, every day.

The kids came rushing back from their latest stop, screeching in delight that these folks gave out full-sized candy bars. It was getting dark, so we paused our conversation to keep our crew closer together. A large mass of people moved toward us, and as our group mixed with theirs, the scene looked like something a comic book creator had come up with while high. I heard someone on the other side of the group whisper, "Dude, I think that banana is my lawyer!"

23

Family Meeting

I SAT IN THE PARKED CAR so long that the windows were now fogged over.

"Mom, are we going in?" Donnell asked from the back seat.

I checked the time on my phone. I'd procrastinated so long that we were about to be late. "Yes. Okay. We're leaving now. Grab your backpack."

We walked across the gravel parking lot in the cold November air, both of us stuffing our hands into our jacket pockets for warmth. I was here to drop Donnell off at school and to tell the administrators that we were withdrawing him to homeschool.

When we'd gotten the letter informing us that he was accepted into this charter school, we'd been elated. When we took his kindergarten first-day-of-school picture, all his clothes bright and clean, it was comfortingly familiar. Joe and I both went to public schools, and so it felt like we were sending our own children off into a system we knew how to navigate.

Even when the first problems arose, we tried to ignore them. Every night Donnell came home with over an hour of homework, almost all of it busywork that reviewed concepts the class had already mastered. We told ourselves that that's just how schools do things these days. A few weeks into the semester, the workload increased further. ("I just played with blocks and ate applesauce when I went to kindergarten!" Joe exclaimed in exasperation as he sifted through the latest stack of assignments.) On top of that, the school was a twenty-minute drive from our house with no bus service, and the commute was starting to wear on everyone.

The problem was that we couldn't find a better option. Our local elementary school wasn't a good fit for different reasons, and we couldn't afford Catholic or other private school. At one point, Joe brought up homeschooling. I laughed. But it was a forced laugh, because something felt right about it.

The more we looked into it, the more it made sense. There were endless options for online schools and classes where we could connect with great teachers from all over the country. The customization of the curricula and the flexibility of schedule worked well for the family vision we were crafting. Yet even as I grew increasingly excited about this possibility, I didn't view it as a perfect solution that would make all of our problems disappear; I had come to see that there are no magic bullets when it comes to making these kinds of lifestyle choices. The name of the game is to take an honest look at the pros and cons of each option, and then figure out which one your family is best equipped to deal with. For us, for now, that was homeschooling.

I nervously stepped into the front office of the school, which was decked in brown and yellow streamers in anticipation of Thanksgiving. The administrator was working to fasten a cardboard cutout of a turkey to the wall when I asked if I could get the withdrawal paperwork. I'd spent my whole life so immersed in the traditional school system that this move felt dangerous and illicit, like I was here to announce that I was kidnapping my child. I'd prepared a convoluted speech about why we'd made this decision, but I didn't need it. The administrator paused her work on the turkey to grab a thin stack of forms from a file and wished us well as she slid them across the desk.

That night, after Kate went to bed, we called a family meeting. For the first time, we would bring them into the discussion that began under the elm tree at the Tex-Mex restaurant. The kids were only now at ages where we could begin to have these kinds of discussions: Donnell had just turned six, Lane was four, Lucy was three, and Kate was one and a half. Even the big kids were still a little young to grasp it all: when we asked them to name three adjectives that describe our ideal family culture, we got answers like "princess" and "ice cream." We set our standards low for the conversation, our only goal this time around to initiate the concept of these sorts of family talks, and to tell the kids about some recent decisions we made.

We had already talked to Donnell in detail about homeschooling, so now we informed the girls. Lucy wandered off to play with the dollhouse; Lane reported that Jarman, her imaginary friend, said he liked the idea. We took that as an indication of assent. Then we told them about my book plan: I was going to rewrite the manuscript, with a goal of finishing the whole thing within eighteen months.

The sting of Ted's rejection of the first draft had faded, and not just because of the passage of time. Seeing my own work as just one part of our family symphony helped keep my ego in check. I mean, I still wanted to collapse dramatically onto a fainting couch every time I thought of the moment I learned that I was facing a full rewrite, but now I had a bigger vision into which I could channel that angst.

And so we explained some of this, in very basic details, to Donnell and Lane (with Lucy half-listening from over at the dollhouse). For the first time, I brought them into my love of writing. My face was bright and hopeful as I talked about how this work filled me with energy. I told them about Ted's rejection, and they gasped as if I were recounting a fireside ghost story with a flashlight under my chin. I explained in my perkiest voice that we should see those kinds of setbacks as *opportunities*, not failures! (I avoided looking at Joe during that part, since I knew he'd be laughing at the irony of me delivering that particular nugget of wisdom.)

The kids were giddy. A little bit of healthy pressure always brings fresh energy into a house, and they were elated to be part of such a crazy, risky endeavor. Donnell promised to say extra special prayers for me. Lucy kissed my hands to bring them good luck while I was writing. Lane gave me her special cross bracelet that had magic powers because the Easter Bunny blessed it on Good Friday, which filled me with gratitude and a desire to pay extra attention to our homeschool theology curriculum.

When I looked at their faces arrayed around the table, so innocent and open and willing to go along with whatever crazy idea their parents concocted, I felt like I might explode with love for these little people.

24

A Beautiful Home

IT WAS TIME TO HIRE A BABYSITTER. We'd had that discussion about the importance of help almost a month before during our trick-or-treating walk, and I hadn't taken any action. When Joe would ask about the holdup, I had a new excuse every time.

"Why haven't you hired a babysitter, Jen?" he'd ask.

"We can't afford it."

"We made that whole spreadsheet about how cutting back on groceries and a few other expenses will make it work."

"If we're going to have someone here for the long-term there are probably tax implications, and who knows how to figure that out?"

"I do."

"Well, I doubt there's anyone out there who'd want to watch this number of kids for the hourly rate we could pay."

"Have you looked?"

"It's more of an intuition."

After one such go-round, Joe finally interrupted and said, "I don't get it. When we worked together, you seemed to thrive when you had a complicated problem fall into your lap. You took it as an opportunity to innovate. Yet now, when you're in the same situation at home, you seem paralyzed."

I opened my mouth to argue but shut it when I realized he was right. If I were working at a company and had to hire an assistant on a small budget for a difficult job, I would have brought my A-game to the task. I would have unearthed previously hidden resources, found a unique angle to attack the problem, and ultimately completed a seemingly impossible job. Yet now that I had a similar conundrum in my home, I was flailing around like a helpless damsel who'd never faced a hurdle in her life. It didn't take much analysis to see what was at the root of it: fear.

This time around, we weren't looking for a temporary sitter. We were hoping to find someone who could come two or three afternoons per week over the long term. But what if I ended up not clicking with her and everything was awkward? What if she was as revolted by our lifestyle as Terri, the babysitter of doom? What if she didn't supervise the kids the right way? What if this really was a self-indulgent expense?

A nun once told me that her number-one rule in life was *Never make decisions out of fear.* That advice had never steered me in the wrong direction, and yet I was completely ignoring it here.

And so I set out to rediscover my energy for solving tricky problems. I felt like a superhero who'd pulled her uniform out of a pile in the corner of her closet, snapped it in the air a couple of times to smooth out the wrinkles, and donned it once again. That version of me who had the burning will to smash past obstacles had been missing for a very long time. Now, she was back.

First of all, I brainstormed with Joe about where I could hire someone who would be a "cultural fit," as we said back in the tech world—in other words, someone who wouldn't look like that guy in *The Scream* painting when she saw that we had almost a half dozen young children in this house. I had just joined a homeschooling list which had many large families as members, and I realized some of them might have older children who were looking for babysitting work. I posted a job offer there.

To make up for a low hourly rate, I offered a flexible schedule and limited the responsibilities to childcare only—no extensive cleaning, laundry, or errand running would be necessary. I also added that the person was welcome to catch up on school work (or read, text friends, or whatever) if the kids were asleep or having quiet time. The other thing I could offer was a bonus internship: I would happily share what I knew about writing or the tech industry, and this person could put it on her résumé and use me as a professional reference.

After a short interview process, I hired a seventeen-year-old young woman named Monica who was the oldest of seven children. She would come three afternoons per week.

When she arrived for her first day on the job, Kate answered the door wearing only a diaper, with Lucy giggling behind her. Lane was having a Barbie doll party in the living room, but we'd lost their clothes long before, so all the Barbies were naked. One of them didn't have a head. Donnell was overtired and had gotten frustrated by a video game so he slammed the remote control on the ground just as we walked into the living room.

I took her on a tour of the house, peppering my explanations with commentary like "I don't know why that shoe is hanging there," and "Is that an apple under the TV stand?" Then we reached the top of the stairs. It must have been my habit to pause right there to point to the three bedrooms because we ended up standing exactly where Terri and I had stood on her first tour. I was in the middle of a rambling excuse for why all the rooms were so messy when Monica's face lit up in a warm, generous smile. "Mrs. Fulwiler," she said. "You have a beautiful home."

Monica was working out wonderfully. Not only was I back to work on the book, but I'd been offered a paid blogging gig with a newspaper called *The National Catholic Register*, which most people referred to in shorthand as *The Register*. It was a popular publication in my circles, and my inbox was flooded with notes of congratulations when they made the public announcement that I was joining the team. The pay was not huge—it didn't even come close to being a four-figure monthly income—but the work was pleasant, I could do it on my own schedule, and it helped me build an audience, which would be important for when Ted started to talk to publishers about my book.

As the weather grew cooler and fall turned to winter, I felt my first big crunch. I was making great progress on the book rewrite. Then, *The Register* asked me to put together a few extra pieces for a special occasion. Meanwhile, Monica was out of town with her family, and I was struggling to keep our homeschool organized. In the midst of all of this, a ministry commitment rolled around.

I generally didn't volunteer for any extra activities. I'd even reached a level of maturity where I could simply say, "I can't take on any additional commitments right now," rather than pretending not to see emails or faking illness like I used to. But I had signed up for a group at our parish that took turns cooking for our pastor and his associates, who worked day and night to serve the thousands of families who attended our church. I only had to provide a night's worth of meals once every six weeks, so it seemed like a reasonable commitment. I actually looked forward to giving back in this small way.

This time, it wasn't working.

As my week to cook drew nearer and my stress level grew higher, an idea kept coming to mind: *What if I asked Papaw if he wanted to do it this time?* I kept talking myself out of it on the grounds that I didn't want to burden him, but the thought wouldn't go away. I had learned a lot of lessons about asking for help in recent years, starting with the time that Hallie came over and ended up dealing with the poopacalypse, and, more recently, my experience with Monica. Combined with Fr. George's insights about letting go of individualistic thinking, I was starting to see that being completely self-sufficient wasn't necessarily a virtue. In fact, my constant insistence on being able to handle everything on my own, with no assistance from anyone, was usually rooted in pride more than anything else.

So I called Papaw and explained the deal. I was in the middle of saying "no pressure at all" for the third time when Papaw interrupted.

"Jenny, would you let me do this?" he asked in his quiet, sincere voice. "I would need about a week to get it all together, but if you have that time, I would love to do this very much. Very, very much."

When I went to pick up the dishes from him a week later, he had pushed himself to the very limit of his energy. He was sitting in a chair in the kitchen when I arrived, and I knew he was worn out when he didn't stand to greet me—an unthinkable gesture to a man of his generation. My dad was coming to stay with him the next day as part of his now-weekly visits, and he wouldn't be arriving a moment too soon. And yet Papaw's face shone with the happiness of a much younger man as he explained each of the dishes.

"The Cornish game hen roulade would be best reheated in an oven at 350 degrees," he said slowly but with great confidence, leaning forward onto his wooden cane. "The vegetable soup was already in my freezer from last month. I hope the padres don't mind."

I assured him that they wouldn't, noticing how he referred to the priests with casual familiarity, calling them *padres*. Though my grandfather was a lifelong Methodist, he had had a lot of exposure to Catholicism in his years in Mexico and South America. He'd always had positive interactions with priests and considered it an honor to be asked to cook for them.

"For the apple crisps I made a graham cracker crust from scratch," he added, pointing to the foil-covered ramekins on the counter. "I looked through my favorite dessert recipes and thought they might like that one the best. I learned about that crust from one of those French chefs on TV. It's really something else."

As I packed up the various dishes into the canvas cooler bag I'd brought with me, Papaw said again, "Thank you for letting me help."

Something in his voice reminded me of the last interaction I'd had with Monica before she'd gone on vacation. She seemed almost worried that this job might not be here when she got back; on her way out the door, she paused to thank me for hiring her. I was so caught off guard that I wasn't sure how to respond. Before I could speak, she explained that she was trying desperately to save up for her own car, but it was hard to find work that would fit into her school schedule. She said that she had been praying every day for weeks for an opportunity like this one.

"Thank you for being my answered prayer," she said. She began to walk to her car, then stopped. She turned around and wrapped me in a hug.

Those words echoed in my memory as I looked at Papaw, who exuded joy through his weakened physical frame. I told him how much this would mean to the priests—they'd be dining on frozen pizza tonight if it weren't for his efforts. And I also told him how much it meant to me. He seemed so moved that I thought I saw tears in his eyes.

"I can't tell you," he said, then paused for a moment before he finished. "I can't tell you how much it means to me to feel needed again."

25

Advent Rock

ADVENT HAD BEGUN, Christmas was just a few weeks away, and I was ready to win this holiday season. Granted, special occasions had led to some of my most spectacular failures as a homemaker, like the time our ginger bread house turned into a ginger bread condemned building. (It looked so terrible that the kids wrote graffiti on the walls in icing to complete the motif.) But I was floating around on a high of optimism since everything had been going so well lately.

After seeing pictures all over the internet of elegant houses dripping in seasonally appropriate decorations, I had great visions of what we might be able to do this year. My creative juices were flowing when Joe returned from the attic and plopped down a beat-up cardboard box on the kitchen table. Its label said *Advent Stuff?*, the words scrawled above crossed-out labels like *Halloween Inflatable Ghost* and *Blow-Up Easter Bunny*, a sad homage to the various seasonal decorations that met unfortunate ends in the Fulwiler house.

I was enough of a realist to know that there would be no handmade wreaths adorning the front door, no garland gracefully draped around the fireplace. A lot of people I followed on social media got an Elf on the Shelf and pretended that he scurried around and made mischief while everyone slept. I skipped that one too for reasons that were explained well by a commenter on my blog who said, "The creators of this thing obviously never saw *Poltergeist.*"

But one decoration I knew we could handle was our Advent wreath, a simple tabletop circle of greenery containing four candles. I pulled back a flap of the box, eager to add this lovely holiday piece to our home. Joe reached in to grab the candlesticks, and out came the most pitiful sight I'd ever seen—and an important lesson that one should not store wax objects in one's attic if one lives in Texas. The summer heat had withered the long candles to the point that they were almost unrecognizable. The wax had seeped down upon itself like sagging skin, and the once regally straight shafts now drooped over like misshapen *L*'s.

In an unfortunate moment of man-think, Joe declared cheerfully, "They're a little melted, but they still work!" He grabbed a match and lit one of the purple ones. We stood there for a long moment, him looking from the burning, lumpy mess to me, realizing that this demonstration was not having the desired effect.

He blew out the candle and tried a different approach. "We can use the white candles in the pantry. It doesn't really matter if they're purple and pink. The colors are supposed to symbolize sacrifice and penance. *Any* decorations we put up in this house are an exercise in sacrifice and penance."

Again, I didn't even answer.

Finally, he said the right thing: "I'm going to go set up the Advent calendar. You handle this however you want."

I pulled the wreath from the box to find that it had also not done well in the furnace of our attic. The plastic pine needles were matted and bent, with hardened drips of wax caked throughout. I pushed the bedraggled candles into the holder at the center of the wreath, hoping to make the best of it, but it was too pathetic. I huffed over to the pantry and replaced them with the white ones, silently lamenting that this wasn't even a real Advent anymore. The Christ child's appearance on earth had been rendered meaningless by the incorrect pigmentation of my candles.

Joe returned from setting out the wooden calendar and nodded approvingly at our attempt at a seasonal wreath.

"See, those candles look great," he said. Then he added: "We can't light them, of course."

I began to object, but then I remembered last year when I turned my back on the fourth Sunday of Advent to see that all of the newly lit candles had been yanked from the wreath and were now being wielded by various toddlers, like the beginning of a very strange fire-breather act.

That evening, I tried to salvage the first day of Advent by reading a seasonal book with the kids. As soon as I announced this idea, I was overcome with the usual sense of doom that befell me any time I contemplated reading with young children. I'd seen the studies about how kids whose parents read to them would all grow up to be nuclear scientist humanitarians, and how kids whose parents didn't read to them would be lucky if they could spell their panhandling signs correctly. Joe and I both read incessantly; I was building an entire career around the written word, for goodness' sake. But reading books to multiple young children was, to me, the type of activity that always made me feel like I'd lost a bet.

Nobody could ever agree on what book to read. After the nightly battles over which title would be our story of choice, new arguments would erupt about who sat where. Then there were arguments about who would turn the page. Then someone would get bored of the story halfway through and demand a new one, and factions would develop over whether to stick with this book or switch to a different one. This night was no exception, and it ended symbolically with Kate throwing a book about God's mercy against the wall.

The next day, I called Hallie to rehash everything. She and her family had ended up moving out of state, and now they lived in Alabama. The move had had surprisingly little impact on our friendship: with so many young children (she now had five), we found it almost impossible to get together even when we lived in the same place. Now we talked on the phone at least once a day. I noted only half-jokingly that if she hadn't told me they moved, it probably would have taken me a few months to notice.

When she answered the phone this time, I didn't even let her speak before I launched into a rant. I pointed out that basically all traditional holiday items are breakable, flammable, traditionally stored within the reach of small children, or all of the above.

"Evidently we cannot handle this kind of thing in our house, so it's time for some new traditions around here!" I declared. "You know what we're getting next year? An Advent Rock."

I laid out a vision of a holiday tradition that the Fulwilers could actually deal with: As Christmastime approaches, families will prepare by getting out a rock. This rock symbolizes the strength of God. Or the stability of the Church. Or something. The Advent Rock would be stored in a titanium cage and hung from the ceiling.

"Hey, the cage could symbolize God's care of us, and hanging it up high could symbolize our desire to be closer to heaven!" Hallie said, the first words she'd been able to speak in this conversation. "I think my family needs one of those, too!"

I sighed into the phone. We'd just finished lunch, and the kids were playing at their sand table outside. I popped a half-eaten chicken nugget into my mouth, then spit it out when I tasted that it was soggy. I didn't even want to think about why it might be waterlogged.

"Okay, but seriously, I worry that my kids will look back at their childhoods and feel like they got short shrift. This always happens this time of year. Maybe God was calling me to have lots of *cats*, not kids, and I misunderstood."

"Just because your first day of Advent didn't go perfectly?"

"Hallie. It was beyond a little imperfect. These candles were just melted blobs. And we couldn't even finish the story about God's mercy before I started threatening everyone for fighting over the book." I explained that I'd come a long way toward accepting the unique way that we do things as a family, but there was still something missing.

"Maybe you need to find a way to be a great mother, but also to be you," Hallie said.

"Did you get that from Dr. Phil?"

"I think it was Pinterest. But seriously, have you ever thought about the unique things you can offer your kids that other people couldn't?"

"If they've ever hoped to see someone sit in a silent room and stare at their computer, they are so lucky to have me as a mom."

"Seriously."

I was about to make another joke, but then an idea popped into my head.

"Hey. Wait. What about electric candles?"

"What?" I couldn't tell if Hallie was asking for clarification because her children were making whooping noises in the background and she didn't hear me, or because she had expected another sarcastic comment.

"Okay, maybe the Advent Rock isn't the final solution. But what if I just did battery-powered candles instead of real ones?"

"Oh, I love that! I just saw some electric tea lights at a Christmas party, and I had no idea they weren't real until someone pointed it out."

It seemed like an insignificant idea, but, for me, it was an epiphany. That night, I went online and found plastic votive candle holders in the traditional pink and purple Advent hues. The plastic was so strong and clear that it looked exactly like glass—nobody would know the difference until one got thrown across the room and it didn't shatter into a thousand pieces. I added a package of battery-powered tea lights to the cart and placed my order.

When they arrived two days later, I cleared off the table. Right in the center, I set down two purple candle holders, then a pink one for Gaudete Sunday, then a final purple one. I switched on four electric candles and dropped each one into place. I remembered that we'd found a green placemat in our *Advent Stuff?* box. I'd been planning to toss it, but now I retrieved it and slid it under the candles.

I stepped back to behold my table. The votive holders looked even more elegant than I'd expected them to. Their exteriors gleamed like polished crystal, and the green placemat evoked the image of a wreath. The tiny lights danced erratically inside as if whipped around by an imperceptible breeze. One day, I would have a gorgeous Advent wreath with real candles whose flames sent light wisps of smoke floating up toward the ceiling. But right now this would have to do; and, in fact, I couldn't imagine anything more beautiful.

That night, I started to read another book with the kids, but it degenerated in all the predictable ways. We were at the part where little people were yanking books around dangerously close to my face when I called a stop. Obviously, I was missing whatever skill other mothers had to make this activity pleasant and not dangerous. But surely there was something I could do here. I did love words. I did love stories. And so I made an announcement.

"Guys, put the books away. We're doing something different tonight."

"We're having a dance party?" three-year-old Lucy asked hopefully.

"Let's do karate!" Donnell jumped up and gave the air a firm chop with his hand.

"Umm, no. No dance parties. No karate. But if you guys will all get in bed, we'll turn out the lights, and I'll tell you a special story that's created *just* for you!"

The kids cheered at such an exotic idea. Donnell rushed back to his top bunk, Lucy settled into her spot below, and Lane snuggled under the covers on her bed across the room. Kate needed my help climbing into Lucy's bed, where she sat up in eager anticipation of her special tale.

"And you guys get to name the characters, too. First of all, there's a princess. What is her name?"

"Arancella!" Lane shouted. A fight almost broke out over Lucy and Donnell having different suggestions, and it occurred to me that I'd have to let them all name someone.

"Lucy, this princess has a dog. What is his name?"

"Pee-Pie."

"Pee-Pie? Umm, okay. Donnell, give me another name."

"Zaranzo!"

"Wow. You guys are very creative. And Kate, do you want to name the kitty?"

"Cat!"

"These are excellent names, guys. Okay, here we go. Once upon a time . . ."

I set the scene for the life of Her Royal Highness Arancella, a spunky princess from a magical kingdom. The ideas flooded in, one after another. Arancella was on a journey. Her dog, Pee-Pie, had been stolen. Her cat, Cat, wanted to help her find him. Christmas imagery floated before me, and I decided that she was following some sort of sign in the sky; instead of a star, it would be a little glowing fairy named . . . Zaranzo.

For years I had thought of my overactive imagination as a defect in my personality. It was my tendency to live in my head that left me twitching and running to check email when I saw a mess on the kitchen table, that made me have to remind myself to hug the people I loved instead of just ruminating silently on their positive qualities. Now, for the first time in years, it felt like a gift.

This world that I brought my children into was magical and real. My mind was so alive with possibilities that the only challenge was cutting down the options to form a coherent story arc. I leaned forward to whisper key parts, then leapt up and waved my hands as I described the great battle where Princess Arancella and Cat summon their courage to fight the wicked witch who'd stolen Pee-Pie. When I brought the story in for its dramatic conclusion, the kids exploded into cheers and applause.

26

Resistance

JOE HAD TAKEN THE KIDS ON A HOMESCHOOLING FIELD TRIP, which gave me some much-needed time to catch up on the book one morning. Just as I began a new chapter, out of the corner of my eye I saw a silver minivan ease to a stop in front of our house. My hands dropped from the keyboard and I began smoothing and pulling at my clothes self-consciously.

My visitor was a woman named Christy, and she ran the meal ministry that cooked for the priests. It was my turn to cook again, and Papaw wasn't feeling up to it this time, so I was on my own to get everything taken care of. When she heard I was nearing the third trimester of pregnancy she offered to pick up the food from me and take it to the church. After all of my recent lessons about accepting help, I silenced the protest that bubbled up within me and simply said, "That would be wonderful. Thank you so much."

The women in our parish spoke of Christy with awe and deference, as she was known to possess more parenting and household skills than all of us put together. She was the one whose children were always immaculately dressed and perfectly behaved in church. Other moms whispered that they'd seen the inside of her minivan and it was as clean as if she'd just driven it off the lot. There were legends that she could do glitter crafts with her children without screaming even once. I had always avoided her, not out of dislike, but because I knew I'd feel inferior in her presence.

As I watched Christy and her three children walking up the stone path through my front yard, hurrying toward the door to get out of the January air, I remembered that I didn't even have the food ready for her. I'd been so focused on my book that I had forgotten completely.

"Heeeeey!" I said when I opened the door, my voice trilling up so high that it broke. I cleared my throat and continued in a normal tone. "Hey, come on in!"

She greeted me warmly, each of her children looking me in the eye and offering appropriate greetings. Her short-cropped blonde hair was sleek and styled, and her white wool pants, inexplicably, did not have a single stain on them. Christy's kids got to work exploring the toy options in the living room, occasionally exchanging perplexed glances when they picked up one toy after another whose batteries were dead. A messy pot of chili simmered on the stove with mismatched Tupperware containers strewn across the countertop nearby.

"I'm so sorry I didn't already have this together. It'll take me just a sec here," I said. The truth was that I felt like my brain was going to melt and I had no idea where to start.

"Why don't you sit down, honey," Christy said. "You're pregnant. Let me get all of this together." I gratefully accepted her offer, watching in awe as she glided from one task to the next. She moved about my kitchen as if she'd lived here for years, quickly locating a ladle to stir the chili, whisking the corn bread out of the oven at just the right time.

While she was dumping the salad into a gallon plastic bag, she said, "My sister sent me a link to that article you wrote for *The Register* the other day. I saw what you said about how all women— even women staying home with kids—need to have an outlet to use their talents."

I'd been enjoying taking all of my ruminations on those subjects and posting them online, but I wasn't prepared to discuss them in person, especially with this supermom who likely disagreed with me.

"Oh, I could be off base with that stuff. I don't know," I said. I hoped to make it clear that my comments weren't meant to be judgmental of her own life choices. "I really respect women for whom motherhood is enough—like you! It probably says something bad about me that I always have to run off and stare at my computer."

"No, Jennifer, that's what I loved about it," she said. She'd had her back to me as she worked at the stove, but now she set aside the food and turned around. "People see that I like to keep my home super clean and I love getting the kiddos all dressed up. They hold me up like I'm doing all of this only out of some really strong sense of duty. But let me tell you, that *is* my thing that I love to do. What was that term you used for it?"

"Blue flame."

"Yes. That's it. Before I had kids I was an interior decorator. Style, beauty, all that stuff—it's my blue flame. I'm using my gifts just like you are."

"Wow. I'd never thought of that before." She returned to her work with the food, and I let her words sink in. Christy was using her blue flame too; it just looked different because her gifts had a natural outlet in household work.

I used to think there was a rare, special group of superwomen who could do nothing but serve their children and their families 24/7, who never yearned to use their God-given talents. Now I wondered if perhaps every thriving mother pursues her personal passions. I thought of the woman in the bookstore coffee shop who'd triggered such insecurity in me years before because she was spending time with her daughter while I was blogging. Maybe she was doing work that she loved as well. Maybe she had a passion for education and felt alive when she browsed the children's reading section. Maybe she was no more or less dedicated to her children than I was to mine. And maybe I could have gotten to know more women like this over the years, and learned a few things from them, if I hadn't thrown up walls between us out of a misguided sense of inferiority.

Progress on the book was good, yet I was surprised by how difficult almost every single writing session was. I'd sit down in front of the blank page, brimming with inspiration, then I'd type a few sentences and think, *This is the stupidest thing anyone has ever written.* I'd see a blog post by a writer whose talent far exceeded mine, and I'd decide that I should give up on the written word altogether, perhaps not even attempting to jot down the grocery list anymore. Social media would lure me away with the siren song of new updates and funny jokes, and I'd find entire writing sessions gone before I even realized what was happening.

If this were something I was meant to do, shouldn't it be easy—or, at least, easier than this? I wondered if this was a warning sign that I was doing something wrong. I referenced this latest round of writer drama on my blog, and one of my regular commenters asked if she could send me a book.

I went ahead and gave her my home address, figuring that if she were a stalker who planned to show up at my house, I could actually use an extra pair of hands around here. A package arrived at the end of the week. I ripped it open and pulled out a small, thin book called *The War of Art.* I glanced at the first page just as I put a pan of fish sticks in the oven for lunch; twenty pages later, the smoke detector let me know that the food was done about ten minutes ago. I stayed up until two o'clock in the morning finishing the book that night, then re-read most of it again the next day. It read like a guerrilla warfare manual for anyone who's ever tried to follow their dreams. It was one, long battle cry for us to get off of our couches and start fearlessly putting our work out into the world.

The book led me to a variety of ah-hah moments, but there was one part in particular that changed the way I saw the world. Its author, Steven Pressfield, put a name to the phenomenon of "Resistance."

Though Pressfield was not writing from a strictly religious standpoint, he elucidated the workings of an insidious force he'd encountered over and over again in his work as a screenwriter and bestselling author.

He spoke of this malevolent entity that hates creation and wants only destruction. Resistance is that temptation that leads you to sit back and criticize others instead of following your own life's calling; it's the lost running shoes and malfunctioning alarms that make it so hard to start that new workout routine; it's the fights that break out among well-meaning people in a powerful ministry at church; it's the force that has stopped countless artists throughout the ages, repelling them from their work like two similarly charged magnets.

"Resistance obstructs movement only from a lower sphere to a higher," Pressfield wrote. "It kicks in when we seek to pursue a calling in the arts, launch an innovative enterprise, or evolve to a high station morally, ethically, or spiritually."

I recognized this force of which he spoke.

Early in my conversion process, one of the things I found most fascinating about the Bible was all the talk about evil and demons. Jesus himself regularly spoke of dark forces working in the world, and it seemed pretty clear that he wasn't speaking symbolically. I would have thought this sounded absolutely insane only ten years before, but I had come to know with certainty that these forces do exist and do operate in the world. Pressfield called it Resistance, though it has been known in the Judeo-Christian tradition for millennia. We might have different nomenclature, but we all agreed it's real, and it's powerful.

And, now that I thought about it, I had been pushed back by this force constantly in my struggles to create in any area of my life—both with my work and with my family.

> *You can't follow that call to have more children—you're already failing so miserably.*
> *Why bother writing this book when so many other people are so much better at this than you are?*
> *You need to give up if you can't adhere to a perfect schedule.*
> *Everyone will laugh at you if you put yourself out there.*

With a jolt, I realized that these were the whispers of Resistance. And, as with all effective lies, they contained a grain of truth: I wasn't the best. There were real issues to manage in terms of being a good mother to my children. There were plenty of areas of life I needed to improve. But the dark tone of these feelings that moved through me like a tsunami, leveling any hope or excitement in its path—that was a hallmark of Resistance.

It made perfect sense that women would be particularly susceptible to this force. Archbishop Fulton Sheen once commented that "the history of civilization could actually be written in terms of the measure of its women." Women have always brought critical insights to their culture's public dialogue, when their voices were allowed to be heard. And women who are close to vulnerable life, by being around children or taking care of the elderly or working with those in need, have critically important perspectives. They have a unique glimpse into the human experience that the world desperately needs to hear, so of course Resistance would want to keep them hidden and silent.

With all of these thoughts still lighting up my mind like fireworks, the next week I got a call from Hallie.

"Have you heard about Ann?" she asked, referring to my Canadian blogger friend. Her voice brimmed with excitement, as if she had big news to deliver.

"I know her book came out a couple of weeks ago. Is there something else?"

"Jen, her book is blowing up. I mean, it's *everywhere*. It's all over the bestseller lists, in the media—everyone is talking about it."

"Seriously?" I gasped. I was standing next to my laptop, in its usual place on top of the fireplace. I dashed out a search. The first thing that came up was the *New York Times* bestseller list. And, sure enough, there was the name of the humble farmer's wife who had no idea how she was going to write a book. My brain raced as I attempted to process what I was seeing on the screen, like if I were trying to understand a complicated puzzle. Listed among some of the most famous people in the world, I saw the name of my friend and her book: *ONE THOUSAND GIFTS by Ann Voskamp.*

"Wow," I whispered to myself. I was so astonished I'd almost forgotten I was on the phone.

"I heard about it because I ran into a neighbor this morning who brought it up out of the blue," Hallie said. "She didn't know I'd even heard of Ann. She kept going on and on about the book, saying I had to read it, that she couldn't explain the impact it had on her life. She actually started crying!"

When Hallie and I got off the phone I dashed off an email of congratulations to Ann. I let out a laugh of disbelief when I remembered her worries that nobody would want to hear what she had to say, that her words might not be good enough. I thought of all of the fears she'd had to face down. I thought of the endless guilt and hesitation that so many of us wrestled with as we pioneered this new age of raising children in the internet era, when we had unprecedented opportunities to share our gifts with the world. As I stood there, a shocking thought came to mind. I tried to dismiss it as an overstatement, but it kept ringing in my soul: *Maybe Resistance is trying to stop women from changing the world.*

27

Decibel

THE BABY WAS BORN AT THE END OF JUNE, our fourth daughter in a row, named Pamela. (We were pretty sure that Donnell had now accepted it as a biennial tradition that Mom and Dad went to the hospital and brought home a baby girl.) I had dared to imagine that my experience with this baby might look something, even a little bit, like our experience with Kate. I pictured another daughter who would spend the first year of her life sleeping and quietly smiling at us.

If I had only taken a moment to picture *the exact opposite of that*, I would have had a clearer vision of how things were going to go with our fifth child. Pammy was what parenting experts delicately called a "high needs" baby. She cried when I picked her up, when I put her down, when I offered her food, when I didn't offer her food—any of these scenarios could be occasions of extreme distress for her that would launch her into screaming stretches that lasted for five to ten minutes at a time (and felt like they lasted hours). I mentioned this on the blog and was flooded with endless suggestions, and I tried them all. Baby-wearing, elimination diets for nursing, allergy testing, co-sleeping—no possible baby-soothing stone was left unturned.

By the time Pammy was nine months old, I was convinced that she was the loudest, most screaming-est baby in the world, as well as in the entire history of the world and in any extraterrestrial worlds we have yet to discover. When nothing was bothering her, she was perfectly cheerful. But the minute she had to face a tragedy like having her shoes put on or being offered food she didn't like, she'd lose it.

Determined to quantify my suffering so that I might assist others in pitying me, I bought a decibel meter to prove that this child had a special gift in the lungs department. When the big kids saw it come out of the box, they wanted to play with it to see how loudly they could make noises. Feeling like a pro parent, I closed the garage door and told them to go have some educational fun with it in there. What I had not considered, however, is that there is no way to make a very loud noise that is also a *happy* noise. Donnell, Lane, Lucy, and Kate took turns nearly blowing out their vocal chords, ripping out shrieking terror screams fit for a sequel in the *Saw* franchise, occasionally pausing to giggle. It was the time of the evening when many neighbors were out for walks, and I could only imagine what they must have thought when they passed the Fulwiler Garage of Horrors.

When we finally tried the thing out with Pammy (the opportunity arising when my arms gave out after holding her up for nine consecutive minutes while she played with a light switch), we found that her screams reached 115 decibels. Joe noted that she was violating workplace safety standards, and according to the Occupational Safety and Health Administration she was required to provide us with protective ear coverings. When I detailed this and everything else to the pediatrician, he just laughed and suggested that we nickname her "Decibel." Which was not helpful.

In the midst of this, my progress on the book remained steady. The months were full of distractions and setbacks and always getting a little less work done than I wanted to, but I pressed on as I was able. And then, on a hot August afternoon, I finished the book. Monica was playing Play-Doh with the kids in the kitchen, and I typed the final words with the sounds of children's laughter and plastic cans clunking on the table in the background.

That last page symbolized so much, so many years of dreaming, so many battles fought. I leaned forward to gaze at it, giving myself the space simply to soak in the magnitude of this accomplishment (and then remembered that Ted could always make me rewrite it again, which took a lot out of the moment). I used up the last of a cartridge of black ink to print the draft for Joe, and at the end of the week he returned it with his feedback.

It was a hallmark of our relationship that Joe and I were always direct with one another, and never was this more true than with his edits. He had plenty of encouraging, complimentary things to say: all over the manuscript there were notes like *Wow!* and *This scene is great—so powerful.* And then there were marriage-testing sentences like: *Dragging a bit. Well, actually this chapter drags a lot.* Next to a paragraph that I had found particularly poignant was a scrawled sentence: *No one cares.* A comment that I thought was rather witty, if I did say so myself, elicited the note: *Is this supposed to be a joke? So weird.* There was a chapter that I had imagined would move my reader to profound emotion with its eloquence, and I noticed that there were no comments from Joe in the margins of its pages, presumably because he was using his writing hand to wipe the tears from his eyes. Then I got to the end and saw his note at the bottom: *This whole chapter makes you seem insane.*

It took me almost a week to incorporate his feedback, and then I sent it to Ted. The moment I clicked the *Send* button, I experienced a disorienting mix of hope and dread, excitement and foreboding. On the one hand, I was confident that this was a solid draft. On the other hand, I'd thought that before. Maybe I'd been thrust into a *Groundhog Day* alternate universe in which I would spend all of eternity writing and re-writing this same book.

Ted replied in only two days. He said he wanted to talk on the phone again. Once again, I observed that saying "it's fine" does not require a phone call.

Since I needed to work within our babysitting schedule, I arranged the call for the next afternoon. It was only twenty-four hours away, but it felt like twenty-four days. While I waited, all the moments that led up to this phone call flashed through my mind: Ted's surprise reply to my email just after I'd found out I was pregnant with Kate; the neighbor girls playing Ding Dong Ditch; throwing the binder with the ill-fated first draft on Hallie's sidewalk with the kids throwing up in the back seat; Ted telling me the first draft was garbage while Barney sang *"If You're Happy and You Know It."*

And even before that, there were all of my dreams of writing a book. I remembered sitting with my dad, our chairs pulled up in front of the TRS-80 computer, breaking down the plot lines of our latest stories. I thought of all those times I'd come home from another long day of being the awkward new kid at school, when I'd drop my backpack by the front door and bound upstairs to the computer. My face would exude carefree happiness, often for the first time all day, as I typed a story that might help someone else escape from their own troubles.

For the call with Ted, I sat behind my desk. Usually, I would have locked myself away in my bedroom (or even the closet, depending on where the household noise level was that day). This time I stayed in my home office downstairs, as if Ted would be able to sense how professional I looked and find himself unable to reject a manuscript by such an imposing figure.

My cell phone buzzed on the desk next to me. My stomach felt like I was on an elevator that just lurched into a freefall. I answered the phone. My entire body was rigid as I forced casual chitchat to begin the conversation.

Then he said, "I read the manuscript."

"And?"

In the millisecond that passed before he answered, I closed my eyes and steeled myself for his pronouncement on the work that I had poured my heart into for years of my life.

"It's ready. We can move on to the next steps now."

I hadn't realized I'd been holding my breath until a burst of air exploded from my lungs. "Really? Seriously?"

"It needs revision, but this is a good draft."

"No rewrite?"

"No rewrite."

My plan was to say gracious words in response, maybe even including a witty twist. In fact, I had been rehearsing my confident and professional comments, muttering them animatedly into the mirror as I brushed my teeth or blew dry my hair. But now none of the words would come, and when I tried to speak, I broke into an enormous sob that had been trying to escape for a long time.

Life Party

THAT NIGHT, AFTER EVERYONE ELSE WAS IN BED, I cleared off my desk to make a clean space for the revision process. When I leaned over my chair to toss a handful of junk into a catch-all basket on a shelf behind me, I noticed a large stack of paper at the bottom. It was my first draft, the manuscript Ted rejected.

I fished it out from under a mess of extension cords and packing tape and pulled this first version of my book onto my lap. It had been so long since I'd laid eyes on this—in fact, I thought I'd thrown it away. I flipped through it, shaking my head wistfully at all the memories and emotion contained in these papers. The faded beige splatters across one page reminded me of the time a rowdy game of hide-and-seek collided with my plan to review the work as I sipped coffee. I saw a paragraph and could almost hear the Old 97s song that blasted in my headphones as I wrote it.

What was most striking, though, is how clearly I saw my mistakes now.

"What was I thinking?" I whispered as I noticed one error after another. The difference in quality between this draft and the one I'd just finished was extreme to the point that they seemed to have been written by different people.

For all of these years, I assumed that my work would be worse for the fact that I was trying to balance it with family life. Back when I used to fantasize about my long, quiet days in a house out of the Pottery Barn catalogue, I assumed that *then* is when my practice of the craft would shine. I would be able to follow the rules of the creativity experts and have a regular and uninterrupted work schedule. Then, finally, I would live up to my full potential as a writer.

But as I flipped through the pages of this old draft, a new paradigm took shape in my mind—one in which all of the interruptions due to my family responsibilities might have actually made me better at what I do. I almost always felt pressure to get as much done as I could before someone woke from a nap or had a meltdown, and this made me less prone to fits of procrastination. Back when I worked on the humor essay website when Joe and I were dating, I was able to schedule writing sessions that could go on for hours. Without hard time limits, I churned out longer, more self-indulgent passages than when I was writing within the pressures of family life.

Igor Stravinsky said that "the more constraints one imposes, the more one frees oneself." I'd come across the quote years before, but I only now got it. When water is confined in a narrow space like a tube or a ravine, it will rush forward with power; when it has infinite room to expand, it becomes a puddle. The same thing happens with our creative juices.

If I had had perfect control over my schedule, I would have been a productivity machine. I would have churned out one page after another, nailing deadlines and slam-dunking all of my goals. There would be no pauses in that "perfect" world where my life was the craft. And what these past few years had shown me is that there is great power in pauses, whether they're chosen by you or foisted upon you.

The weeks when I had new babies were times for me to shift gears and forget all about my work. I would immerse myself fully in the intense moments of nurturing vulnerable new life. Then, when I returned to my writing weeks later, I would come back with a fresh, new perspective. I would discover errors that had been invisible to me before. I'd find that many of my old ideas were now richer and fuller after being given some time to grow.

I also used all the little pauses that came up during times of illness or busyness as an opportunity to educate myself. I'd carry around books about sentence structure and story craft, sneaking peeks throughout the day and in the evening before I went to sleep. All of this eventually added up to a substantial body of knowledge, and I now felt like a warrior who'd finally been trained to use her sword.

There is a tendency with anyone who loves any kind of work to fantasize that if you just had endless time for it, you'd be able to achieve perfection in this field. Yet what I'd discovered is that when you put love first, not only does your life improve, but your work improves. The painter makes time to visit an ailing friend and sees a glow in her face that inspires a whole new series of pieces. The songwriter pauses her career to adopt a child and comes back so raw from her experience that she churns out one passionate tune after another. In my case, I faced interruption after interruption in my house full of babies. And, in the process, I finally learned how to write a book.

I thought back to the joy-filled priest, Fr. George, who changed our lives with the advice he gave me at the extrovert retreat. He told me to see my work as only one small part of a greater vision—which means accepting those interruptions and times when I need to step away. I knew even at the time that this would lead to a better life. What I didn't know is that it would make me better at my craft, too.

I was glad I had that realization about the power of pauses, since I had plenty of time to put it into practice in the following months. The final edits Ted needed me to make were taking longer than I thought they would, and he couldn't start pitching the book to publishers until they were done.

Meanwhile, our home life had been utterly derailed when Netflix suddenly removed Pammy's favorite show, *Shaun the Sheep*, from its lineup. The role Shaun played in our house was similar to the role a snake charmer might play in a cobra-infested village. I tried to get her interested in *Timmy Time*, a Shaun spinoff that featured a similarly animated character. When she toddled over to the TV and punched Timmy's face on the screen, life as I knew it was over.

My only solace was in the comments I received when I wrote about this turn of events on my blog, such as:

Amen! We discovered Dora was gone at 4:46 a.m. one morning. The very fact that I was searching for Dora at 4:46 a.m. says it all.

And:

We have been there with *The Wiggles*. And also, if you do a search for it, they no longer have any of their shows, but it will bring up several adult films under the Bikini Babes series. You might be tempted to read the description to find out why this show popped up when you were searching for The Wiggles. Just . . . don't.

As I settled into my new existence of having Pammy repeatedly hit me as she screamed, "SHAUN SHEEEEEP!", I had a thought that probably could have gotten me diagnosed as being clinically insane: *This would be a great time to have a sixth baby.*

We didn't have a car that would fit six kids. We still couldn't quite afford a bigger house. Money was as tight as ever. Pammy was as crazy as ever. And yet Joe and I felt strongly open—even excited—about adding another child to the family.

Part of it was that we were optimistic about money. My writing career was finally starting to get traction. Right after Ted said the book was almost ready, an editor from a respected magazine said he wanted to talk with me about doing a regular column with them.

It would be a bigger commitment than the blogging work I'd been doing at *The Register*, but it would be a much better income, too. Ted was confident that we could find a publisher for the book, and that might help pay a few bills as well.

But the biggest reason behind my peace was simply that I'd come to understand that things don't have to be perfect in order to welcome new people. I'd come to think of life like a party: if more folks show up, it's more fun. It might mean you run out of the fancy hors d'oeuvres and everyone ends up snacking on chips and salsa. Things might get too loud, drinks might get spilled, and the guests might even annoy you sometimes, but nobody ever wished there were fewer people at their event. There might be times in life when the responsible choice is not to let others in—it's not a good idea to host a barbecue if you're, say, currently battling a rattlesnake infestation—but those times aren't as frequent as we think.

I also felt stronger than I had in years, both mentally and physically. In the time since I'd started thinking from a family perspective instead of a purely individualistic perspective, an ironic thing happened: I started taking better care of myself. Back when I had the mentality that my life is fundamentally about me, I saw the self-giving and service that comes with babies and young children as a fleeting season of life. *Just grit your teeth and get through this time of sacrifice*, I'd tell myself. *Soon it will be over, and you'll be back to your real life!*

These past few crazy, intense years had shattered that perspective. Each of the millions of little moments of love had chipped away at my old way of thinking: sipping tea served in china cups with the neighbor girls; seeing the light in Papaw's eyes every time we visited; watching the kids explode with excitement every time a grandparent walked in the front door; congratulating our babysitter, Monica, when she announced that, thanks to this job, she'd finally saved enough to get her own car; and, of course, the endless hugs from short, chubby arms. Like a stream slowly smoothing over rough stones, these moments had eroded my old way of thinking. I no longer thought that my "real" life was waiting for me out there, in the future, when I'd have perfect freedom and control over my days.

And so I had started to take care of my own needs—without guilt.

I'd recently read a book about Mother Teresa, and I noticed something fascinating: the daily schedule she set for her order, the Missionaries of Charity, included a lot of breaks. I was shocked to see that these nuns had dedicated time to tend to their personal needs. Mother Teresa described how she and her Sisters took time for church and prayer every morning, without fail. Then they went out to leper colonies, slums, or the Home for the Dying and Destitute, working for four and a half hours. After that, they would come back for lunch at around 12:30 p.m. Lunch was followed by half an hour of rest because they had been on their feet so long. Later in the afternoon, there was reading and tea, prayer and community camaraderie, followed by another three hours of working with the poor before they ended the day with dinner and prayers.

The needs of the people they served were endless. In theory, the nuns could help more people if they skipped the time for prayer and tea and reading. In fact, if Mother Teresa had run her order the way I'd run my house, she'd have cut out all leisure activities, in addition to breakfast and lunch. She'd tell herself there was no space for relaxation or real meals because there was *so much to do!* Was it because she and the other sisters were selfish, or not really dedicated to serving, that they didn't spend more hours with people in need?

No.

These daily breaks were a direct result of the fact that Mother Teresa saw her whole life as one of service. She knew that she and her sisters would burn out if they didn't have daily opportunities to refill their own cups. You can't put your own life on hold over the long term; eventually, you'll reach a breaking point where you simply have to take care of yourself. And if you perceive that tending to your own needs can never go hand-in-hand with serving, you'll stop serving.

This realization had been building for a while, and when I read these details about the Missionaries of Charity, it clicked. It really was okay to make time for things that filled me up. Along those lines, Joe and I had started taking turns exercising in the evenings. When he got home from work I would head out for a walk, which was delightful as much for the chance to listen to my favorite music in peace as for the exercise. When I got back, Joe might run down to the neighborhood pool and swim a few laps. Just a few years before, I would have agonized about this expenditure of time; now, I saw it as a normal, even necessary, part of a love-first life.

In early fall, I began to feel that telltale pinching in my right leg. Sure enough, we got a positive pregnancy test the next week. Even though such a moment was nothing new at this point, being my sixth positive test in eight years, it was still thrilling. I could have twenty children, and that first moment of knowing that a new life was now inextricably entwined with mine would never be any less momentous than it was the first time.

I was eager to start my blood-thinner shots, not because I relished yet another nine months of stabbing myself in the stomach, but because it was always a relief to get rid of that painful sensation in my calf. But I got a shock when I went to pick up my prescription at the pharmacy: our insurance coverage had changed, and the price tag was now $2,000 for a one-month supply. After some quick calls to the doctor's office, we found that there was a new, similar line of shots that had just come on the market and would be much cheaper. I switched to that brand and was happy to find that it only had a small co-pay.

I began taking the new brand of shots and anxiously awaited the relief of my leg feeling normal once again. Only this time, it never came.

29

Hotel Room Shuffle

THE PAIN IN MY LEG CONTINUED TO BOTHER ME, even after a week of the new type of shots. I probably would have thought about it more, but the discomfort wasn't significant, and I had other things distracting me: I was preparing for my first speaking engagement.

Thanks to my writing at *The Register*, a faith-based conference had asked me to give a keynote talk in which I would share my story. Even though the crowd I was addressing wouldn't be larger than one hundred people, it was a big milestone.

We brought Donnell, Lane, and Lucy to the event, and the youngest two stayed with my mom and Yaya. We couldn't afford another hotel room in addition to the one the conference was paying for, so we had to do the shell game of hiding kids from the front desk when we checked in. (We affectionately called this the Hotel Room Shuffle.) The only problem was that our room was located near the lobby on the ground floor, within sight of the front desk, so we were prisoners once we were inside.

The evening after my talk, I wanted Joe to go with me to the conference reception so I could introduce him to a few people. We took Lane and Lucy with us and walked across the lobby to the event. We left Donnell, our hidden child, in the hotel room to watch a movie. We had packed walkie-talkies, and we gave one to him and took the other with us.

The girls had already gotten ready for bed, so they were wearing pajamas and socks when we made our grand entrance. People stopped to marvel at this strange family with sock-footed kids who occasionally murmured to someone on the other end of a walkie-talkie. I had just begun introducing Joe to the conference organizer when an acquaintance from the blog world dashed up.

"Jen, hi, I hope I'm not interrupting anything!" she said. Her name was Margaret, and she was an established writer in the politics scene. She shared my interest in spirituality and had been following my blog for years, but this event was the first time we'd met in person. She turned to Joe and the organizer to say, "I need to borrow Jen for a second if that's alright with you, gentlemen." She pulled me away without waiting for them to respond.

"I didn't want to say anything before now because I wasn't sure this would work out," she whispered as we walked quickly to the other side of the room. "But I have someone here for you to meet."

We approached a tall cocktail table in the corner where a man in a navy suit and burgundy tie stood clutching a drink in two hands and looking uncomfortable. Before we got close enough that introductions would be warranted, I paused to check in with Donnell on the walkie-talkie.

"Donnell, you good?"

A burst of static preceded his response. "Yeah, Mom. Ten-four. Over and out."

I clipped the walkie-talkie back onto the pocket of my black slacks and approached the table with Margaret.

"John, I want you to meet Jennifer," she said graciously. She nodded approvingly as we shook hands, looking regal with her layered auburn hair that was beginning to show a touch of silver, her neat black dress accented with a yellow silk scarf. "John, this is the woman I've been telling you about. I've been reading her blog for years and I simply adore her writing. Jennifer, John is an acquisitions editor at Salyer Press."

"Salyer Press!" I blurted out very un-smoothly. In a perfect world I would have played it off like I was the sort of industry professional who talked to people from Salyer Press every day, but I was too stunned to think clearly.

"John is an old buddy of mine from college. He's in town for a publishing conference so I told him he had to run over here so I could buy him dinner and so he could meet you, of course. I'll leave you two to chat." And with that, Margaret swept back into the conference crowd at the front of the room.

"So tell me about this book you're writing," John said. He didn't seem overjoyed by this conversation, but I was undaunted. I told him the book was the story of my spiritual journey, leaving out the part about how I had to rewrite the first draft because it was so bad. I mentioned Ted, and he seemed impressed, maybe also surprised, that he was my agent. He asked me to describe my writing style, but before I answered I had to pause the conversation.

"I'm so sorry, I just need to check in with my son quickly," I said, holding up the walkie-talkie. "Donnell, you still good in there?"

"Can I watch an R-rated movie?"

"No, no you cannot."

"You let me watch that one last week—"

"No, it was PG-13. And that was—I'm not going to go into this right now. Listen, Daddy will be back in just a second. Don't start any new movies until he gets there."

"Ten-four."

I turned back to John. "So sorry about that."

He motioned to Joe and my pajama-clad children, who were now waving at us to indicate they were heading back to the room. "I see you have your hands full," he said.

"That's not even all my kids. We left two at home. I'm also pregnant."

He whistled under his breath. "I don't know how you do all this writing with so many kids, but Margaret says she's a fan, so I'd like to see the manuscript."

"You would?" I stammered. I caught myself and forced an air of calmness. "You would. That's wonderful. I do need to make some edits before my agent can send it to you, and with the holidays right around the corner that will slow me down, but Ted could have it to you early in the new year."

A loud electronic screeching blasted from the walkie-talkie on my hip, then I heard Lane shouting, "I'm Captain Underwear! I'm queen of all the panties!"

I felt the moment needed an explanation, so I said, "The kids are back at the room now. This is some game they play where they run around with underwear on their heads." And then I made a mental note never to speak in front of this man again.

I fumbled to turn off the squawking device while coolly maintaining eye contact, but instead I accidentally turned the volume as loud as it would go. Now Lucy's voice exploded from the walkie-talkie, an incoherent barrage of noise that was supposed to be happy singing but sounded like a tortured soul's dispatches from Hades. Then there was a burst of static and Joe said, "I've got it, Jen. We're back in the room." I finally switched it off and turned back to John.

He seemed to be about to ask me a question regarding what he had just witnessed but shook his head almost imperceptibly. "Here's the problem. Please keep this between us for now, but I've accepted a position somewhere else and will be leaving before spring. I can put in a good word for you with my colleague after I leave, but . . ."

"No. I get it. What's the latest I could have it to you for you to review?"

"Mid-February, at the latest."

That gave me four months. Even factoring in the busyness of the holidays, I could do it. "That will be just fine. In fact, Ted will probably have it to you well before then."

I looked him in the eyes and shook his hand confidently like my parents always taught me to. After we said goodbyes and I took his card, I made sure to do my finest "bestselling author" walk in case he was watching me. I barely held it together to say a few goodbyes to Margaret and other folks I knew in the crowd, and as soon as I was out of sight, I broke into a run. I wore a huge, goofy grin as I anticipated sharing this news with Joe and the kids.

I was so swept up in the moment, I barely even noticed that my right calf ached with every step.

By the time the holidays arrived, I had made little progress on the revisions—and Ted couldn't pitch the manuscript to Salyer or to anyone else until they were done. At first I thought it was simply Resistance, but soon it became clear that something was wrong. My energy was sapped beyond what I had ever experienced in pregnancy, which was especially strange since I was in good shape before this baby came along. I was still early in the second trimester, but every time I walked up the stairs of our house, I had to pause and lean against the wall to catch my breath. I stopped taking my regular walks in the evening since I often ran out of steam only a half block away from the house. The pain in my leg never did resolve; I still had that annoying pinch every time I walked.

I railed against my physical limitations, whose exasperating timing seemed to come right when I was poised to bring all of my writing dreams to fruition. This speaking engagement had paid a generous stipend. I now had a contact at Salyer. The book was almost finished. I was still in talks with the magazine to take a prestigious columnist position with them. Over and over again I tried to power through my exhaustion to get words on the page and hit deadlines; and, over and over again, I failed.

My physical weakness made me feel unable to deal with even the smallest challenges. Joe offered to cook dinner and do the entire cleanup, bath, and bedtime routine on his own. The only thing I would have to do would be to give the kids their goodnight kisses, but even that felt like an arduous, complicated task. All of this combined to leave me feeling disconnected from the entire world, like I was a lazy ghost who huffed and puffed around the house. It used to be impossible for me to relax enough to nap during the day; now I used all my babysitter time to sleep.

The big fear with my clotting disorder was pulmonary embolism, a blood clot that starts somewhere else, often in a leg, and ends up in your lungs. This condition was no joke: it could be fatal with little to no warning. But even though I was short of breath, I was pretty sure that wasn't what was going on: I didn't have any other symptoms like shooting pains or coughing up blood—and, besides, I was taking blood-thinner shots every day, just like I always had during pregnancy. I'd seen a general practice doctor for a routine checkup and he'd assured me that it was pregnancy fatigue. I nodded and quietly agreed that that must be it, but with every day that went by it got harder to ignore the fact that something was very wrong.

30

Breathless

"YOU SEEM OUT OF BREATH," my obstetrician said before we'd even finished our hellos. This was his first appointment after the New Year break, and I was desperately happy to be here. My energy level and shortness of breath were now at the point that I had barely been able to drive myself here; if this kept going, I'd be an invalid within a couple of weeks. My plan was to not leave this office until he gave me something that would make me feel better.

"Yeah . . . I don't feel so great."

"Try to speak for as long as you can without taking a breath. Tell me about Christmas."

"It was . . ." I couldn't get out the third word ("Kafkaesque") without gasping for air.

"You need to go to the ER."

"What?"

"Right now. There's one at the front of the building. Do you need a nurse to take you?"

I shook my head about the nurse, but I didn't see why I needed to go at all. You can't get pulmonary embolisms when you're on blood thinners, right?

"I've been . . . taking . . . my shots."

"You need to go now."

The doctor's office was part of a hospital complex that had an emergency room. Normally, I would have made the walk in about three minutes. This time it took me ten. I had to pause every few steps, lean against a wall, and gasp for breath. My condition was worse even than it had been the week before.

When I arrived at the ER, there were two nurses standing in the waiting room to greet me. They had an admissions bracelet ready and slapped it on my arm before I'd even left the entryway. They led me into a triage room where an IV was started the moment I sat on the hospital bed. The nurses and a doctor exchanged staccato phrases to catch one another up on what my obstetrician had told them.

"What is this blood condition you have?" the doctor asked.

"Factor II," I said. He didn't seem to recognize the name, which wasn't surprising. Nobody ever did. "It's like Factor V . . . with a twist. And . . . I'm homozygous."

"You mean heterozygous."

"No. I have . . . both copies . . . of the gene."

"What are the odds of that?" he said under his breath.

"Honey, how many weeks pregnant are you?" a nurse asked.

"Twenty-two."

There was hushed chatter, and then the doctor turned back to me. "We have to do a CT scan."

Joe texted to ask if he should come down, but I told him to wait until we had more answers after the scan. His office was forty minutes away from this hospital, and I didn't want him driving all the way over just to hear another doctor tell me it was pregnancy fatigue.

After the CT scan, I was wheeled back to a station in the main part of the ER, where my bed was separated from those next to me by plastic divider curtains. I'd begun playing around on my phone to pass the time for what was sure to be a long wait, when a nurse swung the curtain aside and rushed to grab my arm with the IV. She pulled off the cap on the tube and injected a clear liquid into it.

"What's that?" I asked.

She hesitated. "The doctor will be here in a second."

No sooner had she said that than the same doctor from before came back in. He had a friendly face with a dark beard and warm brown eyes, but right now he looked stricken.

"It's pulmonary embolism."

"What? But I . . . was on . . . blood thinners!" That useless statement was becoming my mantra, as if this whole situation would fade away if I kept repeating it enough, like Dorothy chanting "there's no place like home!" in *The Wizard of Oz*.

"The radiologist isn't done looking at the results, but you have clots in both lungs. Some of them are so big a layman could recognize them on the scan images. I don't know—" he seemed to decide to not say whatever he'd been about to say. "We're admitting you to the hospital. You should call your family."

By the time Joe arrived at my room, I had so many wires and monitors attached to me that he couldn't give me a hug. We shook hands with mock formality and he sat down in the chair next to my bed. I told him that the doctor said my condition was now stable, and we moved on to discussing the plan for childcare while I was in here. There were no grand emotional statements, no final I-love-you's in case whatever they put in my IV was as effective as those shots I'd been doing. It wasn't our style.

Joe and I were both at our calmest and most reasonable when we were under stress. Back when we were dating, we'd had more than a few screaming arguments, which was probably due in part to the fact that alcohol was one of the food groups in our diet. But I often thought it was also because we didn't have big life pressures to keep us from disagreeing over minutia. We almost never got in arguments anymore, for the same reason that people stuck in life boats surrounded by sharks don't spend much time arguing with one another.

After he left, I was in the room alone except for the nurse who came by to check my vitals every half hour. This could have been an opportunity for me to reflect on the fact that I had narrowly escaped death; I probably should have used that evening in the quiet hospital room to praise God and think deep thoughts about life and the meaning of mortality. Instead, I started freaking out about how my house would ever run without me.

Joe would have to take time off of work. Even then, how could he possibly handle serving breakfast and lunch and dinner in addition to everything else that had to be done? Who would take the kids to their activities? Our mothers would surely provide assistance as they could, but my mom worked full time, and Yaya could only do so much. I didn't even want to think about how we'd pay the pile of medical bills that were undoubtedly hurtling toward our mailbox.

I had a spacious, private room to myself at the corner of the hall. It had elegant, cherrywood paneling and two polished windows; at a glance it looked more like a hotel than a hospital. The window to my right looked out onto the helipad, and in the middle of my worries, the blades of the Life Flight helicopter started to spin. They twirled until they became invisible, and then the body of the craft floated upward as gently as a bubble in water.

For a short moment, I stopped fretting about the details of my life. My attention was transfixed by the graceful movements of the helicopter, and I felt only concern for whoever was on the other end of that flight. As I watched the aircraft shrink into a distant light in the night sky, I stopped all my frantic thoughts to thank God that I was alive to witness this moment and to pray for all the people who were out there in my city, struggling for their lives tonight.

31

Running Under Water

I NEEDED TO STAY IN THE HOSPITAL FOR OBSERVATION, even though I was out of immediate danger. I was not able to breathe any better than when I was diagnosed, so even simple movements like walking to the bathroom required long recovery time. I spent most of my days using the free Wi-Fi to Google my condition, which made me wonder why hospitals hadn't blocked medical sites yet. By the third day, I had convinced myself that I had three different untreatable syndromes, a brain parasite usually only found in east Cambodia, as well as permanent scarring to my lungs that would leave me gasping for the rest of my life. I harangued doctors and nurses with information I'd learned from medical experts like badboybilly94 on various internet forums. The one highlight of my research was when I found a video where a doctor explained how pulmonary embolisms become fatal, and I noticed halfway in that the soundtrack in the background was Snoop Dogg's "Drop It Like It's Hot."

It seemed like the world should hit the pause button until I could get back to running it but, oddly, it didn't. Hardly an hour passed without me remembering something that urgently needed to be done: *The kids need to finish their current math workbooks to stay on track with homeschool. Lucy needs to bring a photo of herself for a project at religious ed class. There's a mandatory parent meeting for the church summer camp this week. Donnell needs to have that song memorized for drum lessons.* I sent Joe a text every time I thought of yet another thing he would need to take care of in my absence. Every time I sent a new message I expected to get a reply that said "new phone who dis?"

One morning, in the middle of another trip down an internet rabbit trail that made me suspect I had both rabies and malaria, an email popped into my inbox. Most of the notes I received these days were well-wishes from friends and family members, but this one was something different. It was a note from the editor-in-chief of the magazine I'd been talking to, saying they'd found a position for me. The job he was offering was actually better than the one we'd recently discussed, but he needed a sample column to take to his board to get final approval.

It was jarring to think about work again. The email brought back that whole situation—the book, the Salyer opportunity, my hopes for my burgeoning career—as if I were an amnesiac who suddenly recalled her old life. A tidal wave of excitement and stress surged through me as I remembered everything that was going on in that arena.

This offer at the magazine would mean that, if it came through, I'd need to leave my blogging job at *The Register*. Honestly, this magazine opportunity felt like a drag in comparison. But it would be more of a true job, and the impressive title that would come with it would certainly open other doors for me as well.

Meanwhile, there was the opportunity at Salyer Press. The acquisitions editor, John, would be leaving in about a month. I hadn't finished the manuscript revisions. I felt like the correct response to all of this would be to say that none of it mattered in the big picture. "I don't worry about silly things like book contracts and job offers at magazines anymore!" I imagined a more spiritually mature person saying. But I had wanted all of this for so long, and I had worked so hard to get it, and it was so, so close to being within my grasp, that even my current circumstances couldn't smother my excitement.

I sat up in my hospital bed and brushed my hair out of my face. I had to make this work; if I missed out on either of these opportunities, they'd go away forever. My fingers zipped across the keyboard as I made lists and plans and goals, but it wasn't long before I became exhausted and had to push the laptop aside to rest. I was trying to make my dreams a reality, but I felt like I was running under water.

A nasty chest flu filled the rooms of the hospital with coughing, wheezing patients. The doctors made the decision to send me home, since I would have big problems if I caught this virus with my lungs in their current condition. Joe arrived to help me pack, and when he walked in he handed me a greeting card. As I slipped it out of its envelope I assumed I'd encounter a get-well message. Instead, it was a sympathy card, the kind you might give someone whose pet died.

With my deepest sympathy, it said on the front, the words in an elegant script over a photo of a field of lavender. I opened it to see that Joe had interspersed his own, handwritten thoughts with the comforting verses that were pre-printed in the card. It read like this:

> *It is hard whenever something is lost LIKE BLOOD*
>   *THINNERS THAT ACTUALLY WORK;*
> *And you find yourself down in the dumps AT LEAST YOU'RE*
>   *STILL HOT THOUGH,*
> *Due to the grief you feel BECAUSE YOUR LIFE TOTALLY*
>   *SUCKS RIGHT NOW,*
> *But you must take hope in the graces of the future AND BLOOD*
>   *THINNERS THAT ACTUALLY WORK.*
> *Let me know how I can minister to you during this time LIKE*
>   *PUNCH SOMEONE IN THE FACE WHO'S GETTING*
>   *ON YOUR NERVES.*

Then, at the bottom, he added:

I LOVE YOU, BABY! WE'LL GET THROUGH THIS!

As usual, Joe knew exactly what I needed. I leaned forward to hug him but got caught in my wires like a bug in a spider web. He stepped away from his work packing my suitcase and walked over to give me a kiss on my forehead.

"I got that card at the pharmacy when I was picking up your new medicine. I made sure they switched us back to the old type that we always used to use."

"I never thought . . . I'd be excited about giving myself . . . a shot," I said, still not able to talk without gasping. I was especially surprised by my excitement considering that they'd doubled my dose, so I now had to give myself shots in the stomach twice a day.

Joe went back over to the table where my toiletries had collected and resumed putting them in my suitcase. "I think we're famous at the pharmacy now. The whole staff gathered around to see who was going to pay this bill."

"Yeah, I bet they don't see a lot of . . . two thousand dollar tabs." I couldn't even think about the fact that that was only for a one-month supply, and we'd need to come up with the money again in a few weeks. Joe made a noise. Was that a laugh? A snicker? "What?"

"It *was* two thousand dollars. Keep in mind they doubled your dose."

"So, wait. That means . . ."

Joe tossed the white pharmacy bag onto the bed. "Take a look. It's really something else."

I grabbed the bag, which bulged with the bulky boxes of prefilled shots. I turned it around to see the folded, stapled stack of papers that included the injection instructions and the receipt.

And there was the total: $4,090.29. For a one-month supply.

"Did this come . . . with a car?" I asked between breaths.

"I think they forgot to mention that a butler administers these shots in a private jet."

"Let's not think about . . . the other things we could do with this money."

"Let's not think about the fact that we don't *have* the money. I put it on the credit card. That'll be a bracing moment when we open that bill."

Our families could help us cover this round, but then there would be another one next month and the month after that. Also, the bills from my ER trip and hospital stay would be coming in soon. A nurse came in to extricate me from my tangle of wires so I could go home. Joe and I sat in silence as she worked, both of us lost in our thoughts.

At the end of the week, I was at my hematologist's office for what I thought was a routine follow-up, when he announced that he had an idea. From the way he delivered this news, I was pretty sure it wasn't a new patient rewards program.

"You need an IVC filter."

"A what?"

"It's a filter that goes in your vena cava to block clots from reaching your lungs."

"Oh, okay. I guess that sounds good," I said, my speech still slow as I struggled for breath. Then something occurred to me. "But how do they get the filter in the vein?"

He rubbed his hands together as if trying to conjure the right words. "Well, that's the thing." Not the start to the answer I was looking for. He went on to describe a procedure that would involve a tube being wound through a smaller vein, then over and into the vena cava. "Normally we'd go in through your thigh, but since you're pregnant it would be best to come at it from the neck."

Through gasping breaths I repeated his words back to him, making sure I understood correctly that he was suggesting that I would be stabbed in the neck by a tube that would go snaking around, deep into my body, until it got near my lungs and heart.

"That's right," he said. "And since you're pregnant, we can't use most of the sedatives we'd normally use. You'll be awake for the procedure."

I tried to find a polite way to say, *There is not even a chance that this will happen.*

"I doubt we can get it low enough to protect all of your organs, but we can at least cover your heart and lungs. That way, if you throw a clot, you'll only experience kidney failure. We'll also have to make sure we position it so that the baby doesn't put pressure on it, since that could perforate the vein."

"Excellent."

"I see that you're resistant to this," he said perceptively. "You don't need to do it this week, but it'll have to be sometime before labor. I'll have the nurse schedule it about a month before the induction."

I stumbled out of the appointment in a daze. I'd driven myself to this appointment since all of the other adults in our family were busy with various childcare duties, holding down the fort since I was still mostly incapacitated. I flopped into the car and took a moment to catch my breath. To distract myself from the details of the procedure itself, I thought of anything else—what to ask my mom to pick up during her next store trip, what Yaya meant when she said in an email that "Pammy washed the dog with my coffee this morning." And then I thought about my work.

The doctor had said this neck-stabbing procedure would take place a month before labor. Between the recovery time and preparations for the new baby, I would get nothing done in terms of book work between then and the delivery; and then, after the baby was here, I would be out of commission for a while. So, in other words, anything that didn't get done before the procedure wasn't going to get done. That was six weeks from now. My deadline for John was four weeks from now, and I had to write the sample column for the magazine, too. I was running out of time.

Lifted Up

THE MEDICAL BILLS WERE NOW COMING IN DAY AFTER DAY, as if we had signed up for an invoice subscription service. I tried to call the insurance company to question some of the more outrageous numbers, but my first attempt ended in failure. The account was in Joe's name, and they would only talk to him, but he was busier than ever.

I came up with a plan to deal with these claims without using his time: I'd pretend to be him. I'd always had a deep voice for a woman. When I watched the video of Donnell's last birthday party, I heard a voice in the background that made me wonder what James Earl Jones was doing at our celebration and why he was being so bossy. It was disorienting to realize that that was *my* voice. So I figured this could work—especially now that I could breathe more easily. This call would be fine.

I closed the door so I could focus on my technique. Sitting on the edge of the bed, I held the insurance form in front of me and dialed the number. After navigating the touch-tone system, I finally reached a customer service representative. I cleared my throat and put on my deepest, most masculine voice and boomed into the telephone, "YES, I WOULD LIKE TO SPEAK TO SOMEONE ABOUT THIS MEDICAL CLAIM YOU DENIED." I sounded ten times more ridiculous than I thought I would. I didn't exactly sound like a woman, but I didn't sound like a man, either. I was like a genderless robot programmed by an incompetent alien race to mimic human speech.

"Certainly," the woman on the other end of the line said. "With whom am I speaking?"

I put on weird robot voice again. "OKAY, YES, THIS IS—" I couldn't do it. This was too absurd. Why did I have to shout when I used this voice? I dropped the whole charade and said in my normal tone and volume, "Jennifer. This is Jennifer Fulwiler."

The customer service agent hesitated just long enough to confirm that she definitely thought that she was on the phone with the most insane person in the world. She told me politely that she could only talk to Joe, and we both ended the call quickly.

I moved slowly over to Joe's side of the bed, where I put this latest claim form on top of a large stack of other bills and papers for him to deal with. We were out of money, my health was still fragile, I could hardly do anything to keep the household running, there didn't seem to be any way to pull together the book or the column in time, and we were about to have another baby in the house. It felt like the wheels of the clown car of our life were coming off.

I had just said goodbye to Monica when there was a knock at the door. As usual, the kids reacted to the sound like mad Pavlovian dogs, arguing and pushing to see who our new visitor was (we hadn't been getting out of the house much lately). I told everyone to calm down since it was just the babysitter coming back because she forgot something. But when Lane opened the door, it wasn't Monica on the porch.

It was Christy, the supermom who ran the meal ministry for the priests. She held a large, foil-covered baking dish in one hand and carried a bulging canvas grocery bag in another. (And, I noticed, she was wearing white again.) Now a second person, whom I recognized as another volunteer cook, trotted up behind her, holding her own canvas bag and announcing that she got the bread. What bread? What was going on here?

Before I could ask, Christy explained. "Hi, Jennifer! Father

Dean emailed us to say that you've been ill. He mentioned that he brought you Communion in the hospital. Isn't he wonderful?" She stepped inside, once again moving as if she were in this space every day. To say that my house looked like it had been robbed would be an insult to robbers. It looked like thieves had broken into the place, intended to rob it, and just got drunk and thrashed around for a while instead. She didn't seem to mind.

"Anyway, the other meal ministry folks and I set up a Care Calendar for you, so you'll have meals every night for the next six weeks."

"Oh my gosh. Seriously?"

"Put this one in the freezer," she said to the lady who was helping her, whose name I couldn't remember. "Word got around and a bunch of other families from church signed up, so it should be quite some time before you need to cook again!"

She adeptly set out a stack of plastic and foil containers with the food for tonight, a roast with sides of homemade garlic mashed potatoes and buttered green beans. There was another full meal for tomorrow, which she stored in the fridge. She wiped her hands on a dish rag she found in a drawer (locating it on her first try), then used it to dab a spot of condensation that the containers had left on the counter. The kitchen was now more orderly than it was when she'd arrived.

She and her helper friend left, after about a thousand thank-yous from me, and I pulled up this Care Calendar thing on my phone. Each week was filled with the last names of people from our parish, each of them choosing a date to deliver a meal. The first two names were women who were in my Bible Charades group at the extrovert retreat.

The next day the neighbor girls came over (knocking, as everyone did, since the doorbell was still out of service from when I'd disconnected it that afternoon years before). They carried two disposable casserole pans, overflowing with their mothers' favorite recipes.

These dishes could easily be our lunches for the next few days. "Is Mr. Joe home yet?" Carmen asked as I was putting away the food.

"Not yet. Unfortunately, he has to work late tonight."

She looked at Megan and Riley for confirmation, then offered. "Why don't we stay and watch the kids so you can chill out for a while? You can go upstairs and read a book or whatever. You don't need to pay us or anything."

I told them they were absolutely angels sent directly from heaven and took them up on their offer. Two days later, they came by to offer their free babysitting services again, then the next week as well. I started making them nervous with the intensity with which I conveyed my gratitude. I'd look them in the eyes for an awkwardly long time, burning with sincerity as I said, "No. Seriously. You do not understand what this means to me." They kept saying they were just happy to help.

On one such day, right before I was about to fall into bed for a nap, I noticed a stack of letters on the side of the dresser. Joe must have put it there after he checked the mail, but I'd only now noticed it. All of it was addressed to me. I tore open five envelopes, each of them cards with well-wishes. Two were from my aunts. Another was from an uncle. Some of them contained checks or cash. I was reading a kind note when the phone rang. It was Hallie.

"Hey, I am getting overwhelmed with requests from your blog readers," she said. Hallie had recently set up her own website where she shared stories and inspiration. Like me, she had found that this creative outlet gave her a whole new source of energy. "I guess people are finding my contact info from my site since they know we're friends, but everyone is asking me to set up a fundraiser to help you."

"Wow!"

"Yeah. I want to do it. Word has gotten around about the cost of this medicine, and people are adamant about helping. Is that okay?"

"That's so nice, but—"

"Don't say you couldn't accept. Honestly, you should read some of these emails. People really want to help, Jen."

Hallie put the fundraiser button up that afternoon, and the donations poured in immediately. I didn't want to watch the numbers too closely, so that I could maintain a mindset of being happy with whatever we were given. I didn't look at the site again until almost a week later. When I did, I shouted so loudly that Joe called upstairs to see if I was okay.

People had given us almost ten thousand dollars.

What was even more meaningful than the dollar amount was the notes. The form allowed donors to include a comment with their gifts, and I was moved to tears as I read through them. Some shared about difficult times in their own families. Some told stories of how something I wrote helped them (or, more often, just made them laugh at the ridiculousness of a crazy situation I'd gotten myself into). Everyone said they were thinking of us and praying for us. I felt uplifted by the love of this community, as if they were physically holding me up.

I once thought of my writing work, perhaps especially the time I spent updating my blog, as a self-indulgent activity. Yet what I saw from this flood of gifts and comments was that what I had done had helped people—not because I had mind-blowing talent or because I had skills that others don't possess, but simply because I had put something out there. I had taken powerful moments in my life, both the poignant and the absurd, and had made my best effort to distill them into words. And, like a photographer who shares an image of something that moved her, or a poet who writes a few lines about what's on his heart, it gave people a new way to look at one small slice of the human experience. In the end, that's what all art does. Even the informal mediums like blogging make us more human and more connected in our shared humanness.

I asked Hallie to take down the donation link, since this would be enough to cover my shots for the rest of the pregnancy almost completely, and that was more than I could have ever dreamed I would get. After the final donation came in I pulled up the list and read each note again, wiping tears from my cheeks as I beheld this unfathomable outpouring of love.

"That Could Have Been Me"

JOE AND I SAT IN THE WAITING ROOM OF MY HEMATOLOGIST, who was running an hour late. At any other office, that news would have annoyed me, but this place was different. My hematologist primarily worked with people who had cancer, so this waiting room had a way of putting everything in perspective.

Joe and I settled in close to one another on a floral-printed couch in the corner. The only other people in the room were a couple in their fifties; the woman wore a colorful scarf over her balding scalp, and she interacted with her husband with cheerfulness. Joe and I kept our voices low so we wouldn't disturb them as we spoke about all the issues we faced. The generosity we'd received had been nothing short of life-changing—but, as we now discussed, even that outpouring of support didn't come close to resolving everything.

"We're in over our heads," I said, as much to myself as to Joe.

I expected him to lean forward and pull out a folded, three-page spreadsheet from his back pocket and start pointing to numbers to illustrate the elaborate plan he'd concocted to get us out of this mess. Instead, he said quietly, "I know."

We held hands, both of us silent. I watched the woman in the scarf say something to her husband. When she looked at him, her glance wasn't casual; she beamed when their eyes met. When she smiled it wasn't a perfunctory gesture; it was a big, wide, all-in expression. She playfully punched him in the arm and leaned in affectionately as she told him a story. He made a brief comment, and she laughed—a hearty laugh that was so bold that both receptionists looked up when it filled the room.

A flicker of desire registered within me—a desire to possess the same kind of care-free joy this woman had—but it was quickly smothered by my worries. I had so much work to do before the vein filter procedure. I was almost finished with the revisions on the book. There was only one thing left to do, but it was a big thing: I had to rewrite a chapter. When that was done, I would need to put together a proposal for Ted to send to Salyer, and that would be a long process in and of itself. On top of that, I needed to write a sample column for the magazine job, and they needed it soon.

I summarized all of this for Joe. He seemed to be half listening, more engaged in watching the interactions between the woman in the colorful scarf and her husband. I had only paused, not even finished with my manic ramblings, when Joe spoke slowly and calmly: "What if you let it go?"

My voice was muted but shrill. "Let what go?"

"This Salyer opportunity. The magazine column. How much less stress would you be under if you loosened your grip on these things and just let them pass?"

"Joe. Come on. These are the kinds of opportunities I've been dreaming about all my life. I'm not going to choke now."

"But is it bringing any kind of joy into your life?" Joe removed his gaze from the couple and turned to me. "It would be one thing if this were giving you energy, like your writing work usually does. But every time you bring up Salyer or the magazine you get all miserable."

"But I need to—"

"Wait. Hold on. Before you say anything else, just stop for a second and imagine giving yourself space to do your work in peace. Imagine telling Salyer and the magazine that you need much more time to get everything done. And if that doesn't work, then you're not the right person for them."

"John is leaving Salyer soon. He's my only contact there. The magazine folks already said that they need to make a decision soon.

For both of these opportunities, saying I need more time is the same as saying no."

"Okay. So what if you said no?"

A nurse opened the door and stepped into the waiting room with a clip board. We paused to see whose name she'd call. It was the lady in the scarf. Her husband supported her with a gentle hand on her arm. Her interactions with him and the nurse were so warm that it was easy to miss how she walked with visible pain. We were silent as she moved across the room, as if watching a holy procession.

Something was changing within me. I could feel it, and I resisted it. Joe's question had removed a stone from a wall I'd built up around this issue, and I was desperately trying to stop the whole thing from crumbling.

"But this is my big dream!" I said, then repeated it again, as if I were trying to convince myself more than I was trying to convince Joe.

"What is your big dream? Working with Salyer?"

"Well, it doesn't have to be that publishing house, but getting a book published? Yes! I've been fantasizing about that since I was nine! Not to mention the fact that I've poured my blood, sweat, and tears into this project for the past five years of my life!"

"Nobody's talking about not seeing this book through. I'm just saying that you might find yourself a lot happier if you tell that John guy that the timing just isn't working out for this particular opportunity."

His words hit me as if I'd been punched, probably because I knew they were true.

"You know, you'll never regret it," Joe said.

I had been staring at the floor, but I now turned to him. Joe had faced similar dilemmas in his own career, only on a larger scale. Just last week we had seen a profile in the *Wall Street Journal* about someone he knew from Yale, a guy who was now CEO of a tech company. His team developed an app that pretty much everyone I knew used, and the article hailed him as a brilliant visionary who was changing the tech landscape.

"So you never miss it?" I asked, my tone softer now. "You never see your friends in the industry news and think, 'That could have been me?'"

He chortled. "No, I do. I think that every time. I say, 'That could have been me. And thank God it's not.'"

"Really?"

"Yes. Absolutely. Look, when we met, I had spent a decade living for my career. It's all I did in my twenties. And when you start getting the big titles and the nice accolades, at first it feels great. But it's easy to get caught up in those externals—the things that impress people but don't ultimately make you any better at what you're giving back to the world. When you chase that kind of stuff, it eventually becomes an addiction."

"And you end up living for your work."

"No, it's worse than that. You're not even really living for the work. You're just using your work as a means to impress people, and you're living for that, for other people's approval. And those people don't even really care about you."

When we'd begun talking, we both sounded defeated. Now, the mood had changed. A palpable feeling of hope enveloped us as we sat in silence, both of us lost in thought.

Until now, I hadn't understood just what this life that I was trying to craft for myself and my family would really look like. I had set out on this quest to try to "have it all," to use the terminology of the age-old debate about women and work. Now that I considered everything I'd learned along with what Joe was saying, I saw the entire concept differently. It occurred to me that you *can* have it all in the sense of having a rich family life and pursuing excellence in your work, but you're going to need to re-imagine what having it all looks like. Your work will never be your number-one priority. You might need to walk away from glamorous opportunities that don't allow you to live a love-first life. You'll be bombarded with one interruption after another, yet you'll find that those interruptions are the very building blocks of a good life.

The nurse now returned to the room and called my name. I stood, but Joe took my hand to stop me. He wanted to say one final thing.

"If you want to live a life where you actually have the energy left over to have real relationships with the people you love, you're not going to be able to say yes to every cool opportunity." He squeezed my hand. "And you'll never, ever regret it."

As I walked toward the exam room, I felt light (which was quite an accomplishment for a woman nearing the third trimester of pregnancy). I felt like my face was as happy and open as the face of the woman in the colorful scarf, lit by the knowledge that I was ready to let go of things that didn't ultimately matter.

That night, I had originally planned to force myself to work on the book. Instead, we declared it family game night and got out Monopoly. (And when more than two hours had passed and only four properties had been sold and our collective will to live had reached its nadir, we gave up and switched to family movie night.)

By the time the credits rolled on the movie, all the kids were asleep, stretched across the couch and piles of blankets on the floor. Joe and I began whispering strategies for getting everyone into bed, but I told him to hold off for a second. There was one thing I wanted to do before we went upstairs for the night.

I retrieved my laptop and set it on the kitchen table. I typed up a draft of an email to John at Salyer Press, cc'ing Ted. I told him that I could have Ted get a quality draft and proposal to him if he could just wait a while, but I knew that wasn't an option, so I would need to pass on this opportunity. Then I wrote another email to the editor-in-chief of the magazine, saying something similar: if he could wait, I could put together a good sample column for him to take to the board. But I knew that they were looking to hire someone quickly. With this email I would withdraw myself from consideration.

Before I sent either one, I set the computer aside and turned to Joe, who was wiping pizza crust crumbs from the table. "You sure about this?" I said. "I don't really see how we're going to get a bigger car or house if I'm not making this push on my career."

Joe dumped the crumbs in the trash and sat down across from me. To keep the kids asleep, all the lights were off except for the dim glow of the bulb above the stove.

"It's not like you're completely shutting down your work. You're just letting go of opportunities that sound cool but are actually ruining your life. Who knows? Maybe something better will come up."

"So you're not worried about money?"

Joe leaned forward and gave me a knowing look. "I'm always worried about money. But I'm more worried about ending up with a life that I'll regret. Remember Robert, the partner at the firm I used to work for?"

We'd recently discussed this man, another person whom we'd seen quoted in national news articles, hailed as a paragon of his industry. "Yeah, I know who you're talking about."

"He just recently retired, and I shot him an email to say congrats. I guess I caught him at the right moment because he responded with this long, really personal message—and this is the guy who used to respond to emails about billion-dollar deals with, like, two sentences."

"Wow. What did he say?"

"He'd heard that I have a bunch of little kids now, and he just gushed about that. He said that he neglected his personal life for his work, and it was his greatest regret. There was this one line where he said something like, 'I didn't understand what actually matters in life until it was too late. Don't make the same mistake I did.' I keep reminding myself of that every time I worry about money lately."

I nodded. There were good reasons for me to push to make these opportunities happen, yet I was filled with a sense that it would be okay if I let them go, even if I didn't see how at this moment. I was slowly coming to adopt the new mentality that when you put connections with other people first, things tend to work out. You might face difficulties. You might experience suffering and loss. Like Yaya in her life as a single mother, things might not look exactly as you hoped they would. But you will never, ever regret putting love first.

While Joe finished wiping down the table, and as he loaded the dishes from our family pizza dinner, I sent both of the emails.

The Drive

JOHN AND THE MAGAZINE EDITOR both got back to me the next day, and both confirmed what I thought: neither could give me more time. Those opportunities were gone. We exchanged polite good-byes and wished each other well.

And in the days that followed, a surprising thing happened: suddenly, I was full of inspiration for the book. For months now, the revision process had been slow and painful. Even the simplest edits left me feeling stuck. I'd open up a page when Monica arrived, and I'd still be staring at the same page when she left. Now, the ideas came one after another.

One afternoon my laptop was set up next to me on the arm of the living room chair. This wasn't a sitter day, so everyone was basking in the late-afternoon lull. I had just gotten Pammy down for a nap, a process which reminded me of a crocodile wrestling video I once saw, except the crocodiles weren't screaming, "HATE NAAAAAAP!" Kate watched a TV show, Lane and Lucy were playing with the dollhouse in their room upstairs, and Donnell was hard at work on a new lemonade recipe in the kitchen.

I was zoning out, half reading an article on a news site, when I was rocked by a huge idea. There was one chapter that had been weighing me down for months. It was the last major thing I had to change before Ted could pitch the book to publishers. I knew it needed to be rewritten, but every time I sat down to improve it my mind went blank. And now the answer for how to fix it was perfectly clear.

I typed as quickly as I could. I'd finished a solid paragraph and was starting on the next when I heard a sound. It was a bang—like, say, the sound a toy would make if it were thrown against a wall by a crazy toddler who had finished her nap early. Like a sailor hearing the rumblings of Leviathan, I knew Pammy had woken up.

I was not about to quit now. Inspiration was with me in a way I'd rarely experienced; I was going to keep riding this wave, and I would bring my family with me. "Guys! Listen up!" I shouted as I jumped up from the chair.

Donnell looked up from his lemonade work and Kate turned from the TV. Lane and Lucy happened to be coming downstairs anyway to tell me that Pammy was awake, and they stood next to Kate, undoubtedly eager to see what could have caused this burst of energy in their mother.

"Okay," I said, speaking as if I were addressing troops. "I am finally making progress on this chapter that I've been stuck on."

"Is that the one that you told us about?" Lane asked.

"Yes. The one I keep talking about. I finally found the solution. And when I'm done with it, I'll be done with the whole book!"

Lucy bounced up and down and clapped excitedly. "Yay Mommy!"

"But here's the thing. Pammy's awake now. You know I can't work on this chapter once she's up, but I really, really want to finish this today! Does anyone have any ideas for what we could do here?"

Their faces lit up, a reaction that I was coming to expect from the kids when I asked them for favors like this one. It always made them feel important whenever we let them in on what was going on in our adult world. A variety of ill-conceived ideas were floated, from giving her a gallon bucket of ice cream and a spoon to going down to the pet store and buying her a kitten to play with (the latter being Kate's suggestion and a sly attempt to get a pet for herself). I asked them if they thought they could keep her from completely demolishing the house if they all worked together to entertain her for an hour or so, and they said in unison: "No."

"HATE NAP!" Pammy shouted from upstairs.

"Wait!" Donnell set down his lemon squeezer. "There is one thing Pammy loves to do that would keep her occupied for you." He glanced toward the front of the house and immediately I caught what he was getting at. The car.

I told the kids to go to the bathroom because we were going on a drive. I got Pammy out of her crib and changed her diaper. When I told her we were going for a ride, she was delighted. I grabbed my laptop and my keys and walked behind the line of kids to shepherd them into the car. Before I started the engine, I made an announcement.

"Guys, we are going to do something crazy. Tell them about your idea, Donnell."

"Mom is going to write in the car!"

"I'll drive to a place where there's something to see, pull over, and then write on my laptop until Pammy fusses. Then we'll move on to another stop. If you guys could help me keep Pammy amused, we'll have an ice cream party when we get home."

Everyone responded enthusiastically, and we set off. Our first stop was the local duck pond. I pulled up alongside the murky body of water that was not even half the size of a football field, rolled down the windows, and turned off the ignition. The sound of quacking drifted in on the unseasonably warm February air.

The kids couldn't get out since I would be occupied, so everyone had their work cut out for them to keep their little sister entertained within the car.

"Look, Pammy, duckies!" Lane exclaimed as if it were Santa Claus himself out there floating in the pond. I turned around to give her a wink and a thumbs up before opening my laptop.

I wouldn't have expected that a minivan full of little kids would be a place of great artistic inspiration, yet the words flowed. Sentences filled one page after another, with seemingly no effort on my part. This chapter that had been torturing me for months now poured from my keyboard as if I were taking dictation. I was in the middle of jotting down a new line when Pammy kicked the passenger seat in front of her, so I set the laptop aside, started up the car, and we took off again. This time we stopped in front of a community pool ("Pammy, it's a pool! Isn't that amazing?" Lucy exclaimed). Next time it was a neighborhood pavilion. Then it was another pond.

"Guys!" I said as we pulled away from the pond. "Guys, I am almost done! I've been getting so many words out on this trip that I'm about to finish this chapter. And when I do, that means this whole final draft is done!"

They all bounced in their seats, shouting words of encouragement. "There's a park somewhere around here that always has lots of squirrels!" Donnell suggested. It was a great idea. We drove over there, and it bought me a solid chunk of writing time while the girls helped Pammy give each animal a name. Now I was getting close, very, very close. At Lane's suggestion we drove over to see a different neighborhood pool. After just a few minutes parked there, I got the final words typed.

"It's done!" I screamed, even more loudly than I'd meant to. "It's done! Five years working on this thing, and THIS BOOK IS DONE!"

The car exploded in cheers. Everyone's arms shot into the air as if they'd been watching a tied football game and their team finally scored. The kids high-fived one another and then me. Pammy grinned appreciatively, assuming all the applause was for her. I turned around so I could see each kid and leaned into the back seat.

"Thank you. Thank you guys so much. This meant a lot to me, and I truly couldn't have done it without you."

When we got back home, everyone was still high from the excitement of the big trip. I served the promised ice cream, and my crew of helpers wiggled and swung their feet in their chairs around the table as they enjoyed their hard-earned reward.

Later that week, I came back downstairs after putting the kids to bed to find the place empty. I'd expected to find Joe working on kitchen cleanup, but everything was finished, and the room was still. Eventually, I found him outside on the back porch.

"What are you doing out here?" I asked. I rubbed my hands against my arms to stay warm.

When he turned to me, his eyes were unusually bright, as if he'd seen something magical. "I just had an idea," he said.

"What was it?"

"What if we got a deck?" He presented the idea the same way he might have presented the option of forming a traveling family Riverdance troupe—as if it were something exciting and outlandish and life-changing.

I didn't follow. "A deck?"

"Come down here so I can show you what I'm imagining," Joe said. He produced a small flashlight from his pocket and led us down the porch stairs and into the yard.

He turned us so we were both facing away from the house, toward the fence that separated our yard from the wild greenbelt area behind it. "Imagine installing a gate so we could get out into the greenbelt easily. We could go for walks, and the kids would love exploring it," he said. We didn't own that land but we had access to it, and making use of it would make our property feel more spacious. "Maybe we could put a fire pit in the yard. Can't you just see us sitting out here and making s'mores while the kids run all over the place?"

Then he had us turn back to the house. Our house was built on a slope, with the level of the yard eight feet below the main level of the house. The landscape was tilted so steeply that it was unusable for anything other than rolling down the rocky hill. One of the tough things about living here was that the only outdoor area where the kids could play unsupervised was our tiny back porch. We looked back up at the house, which loomed above us, and Joe leaned close as he described his vision for a basic deck that ran the length of that side of the house. He painted a picture of the kids laughing as they pushed scooters across the smooth surface, with him tending the grill and me reading a book under a porch umbrella.

I interrupted him to say, "Sure, that's a great vision, but I don't understand why we're talking about it now. This isn't exactly the time to be thinking about home improvement projects, with everything else we have going on."

"What I'm saying," he replied, "is that this is a way we can stay in this house."

I looked at him, then back at the imaginary deck. Now I got it. If we made our outdoor areas more usable, it would help relieve the pressure that came with all of us being cooped up in cramped quarters all the time. Countless mothers throughout the ages had raised big families in tiny houses—and they did it through the power of the sanity-saving phrase, "Go outside!" These changes would give me access to those magic words, too.

"We can't do this right now," Joe said. "But we can save up for it. And it would be a heck of a lot less expensive than getting a bigger house."

Speaking of upcoming expenses, I said, "And the car?"

He shook his head happily. "What if we let go of that, too? What if we decided to get by with what we have? Where is it written that you absolutely have to have a car that fits your whole family?"

I laughed. "I guess it's not."

The house in front of us somehow looked different after this conversation. Lately, I had been so fixated on what I thought we were supposed to have in a home that I had eventually convinced myself that I was dissatisfied with this one. I had never paused to ask myself what actually felt right for our family. Now that I did, I saw that I loved this place. It was small, but it was perfectly laid out. When we stumbled across this house so providentially years before, one of the things that made it seem like an answered prayer was that its details were perfect for us. It had a small kitchen but a spacious, walk-in pantry. All the bedrooms were close together upstairs, so it was easy for us to hear if a kid needed us at night. The dining room had made a perfect home office since it allowed me to stay in the mix of things downstairs while I was working. The back of the house looked out over a greenbelt, which the kids saw as a place of endless opportunity for adventure.

The windows glowed, the light from inside warm and welcoming against the cold, dark night. I thought of all the life that existed in that little space, all the memories that had been made behind those windows. I pushed closer to Joe to stay warm, and he put his arm around me. Right then, I let go of my desire for a bigger house, which, now that I thought about it, had never been a true desire of mine to begin with. I let go of my fixation on getting a bigger car.

And when I did, the pressure floated away, too.

Now I didn't need to worry so much about when I would make more money from my career. Joe could continue doing work he enjoyed and wouldn't have to switch into a high-paying, high-pressure job. I had spent so much time worrying about how we would pay for a lifestyle upgrade, and now all that stress disappeared into the cool night air.

I wished it wasn't so dark, so that Joe could see the joy on my face as I came to understand that we could be happy with what we already have, right now. In fact, we could be *very* happy.

The Night Watch

THE NECK PROCEDURE WASN'T AS BAD AS I'D EXPECTED IT TO BE; it was far, far worse. I had to lie flat on my back at eight months pregnant, which meant that the weight of the baby pressed right on my diaphragm. This, combined with the fact that my lungs still had not fully healed, made it feel like I was slowly suffocating for the entire procedure.

On the plus side, it failed.

The surgeon who performed the operation explained that he wasn't able to get the filter in for some complicated reason having to do with pregnancy. I was overjoyed, since it meant that I wouldn't have to go back in for another tube-snaking-through-my-veins procedure to remove it.

Also, there was no recovery period at all. Contrary to all the images I'd conjured of me lying on the floor, clutching my neck and screaming (I don't know why I imagined that I would be on the floor), I felt the same as I did before the procedure. This meant that I had time to put together a proposal before the baby arrived. It was too late for the Salyer opportunity, but I could get it ready for Ted to send to other publishing houses.

Everything was running smoothly at the house. The neighbor girls were still offering their free babysitting services, in addition to Monica, who still came three afternoons per week, so it came together quickly. When Ted finally said it was ready, I stared at that email for a long time. This was it.

The first rejection came in two days later. Then another, then another. I started to dread seeing emails from Ted that started with

"FW:", since it was always some acquisitions editor talking about why the book wasn't a good fit for them. But then one publisher made a bid. And in the midst of a few more rejections, so did three more. When I realized that we would accept one of these, and it was just a matter of time until we decided which offer to take, I ran screaming into the living room to tell the kids, and they were so excited that it turned into a spontaneous dance party (which was quite a sight since I was eight months pregnant).

Hallie and her family placed a phone order for a full pizza dinner for us that night, complete with a side of double-fudge chocolate mini cakes for all. We called them on speakerphone so they could join in the toast Joe offered for this accomplishment. We could hear Hallie's family cheering from their home a thousand miles away as we all clinked glasses.

The publisher I ended up choosing was a relatively small house, but they were highly respected. Many of the books that sat on our personal bookshelves had their name on the spines.

The more I got to know the team there, the more I saw that they were the perfect fit for this project. Truly, I came to believe that this was the best publisher in the entire world for this book—and I might not have ever discovered them if I had shoved my family's needs aside and grasped at the opportunity with Salyer. At one point I spoke with an editor who said that she found a certain section to be particularly well-crafted. "This chapter really demonstrates that you're a pro," she said.

It was the chapter I wrote in the car.

We were still finalizing the deal when I went in for the labor induction. We were all excited to bring this floundering mess of a pregnancy in for a landing, and we couldn't wait to get home with our new son. Joe and I talked a lot about how we would celebrate the book contract when it finally came in. The baby would probably be about three weeks old, so we could sneak out with him for a quick dinner. We'd go to a nice restaurant and we'd bring a special pen for the signing. With the candlelight illuminating the papers that represented so many years of hard work and three decades of dreaming, I would write my signature. Then I'd order the most luxurious, decadent dessert on the menu.

The baby arrived, and we named him Joseph Thomas. The nurse handed him to me in a blue swaddling blanket, and normally I would have marveled at the novelty of having a baby boy for the first time in eight years, or remarked that he was our first child with blonde hair. But something didn't seem right. He felt cold, and he made quiet grunting noises as he breathed. I only had him in my arms for a moment before he was whisked away by nurses, who came back to tell me that his lungs had not fully developed and had sustained damage during the delivery process. Though his prognosis was good, he needed to be transferred to a Neonatal Intensive Care Unit in a hospital thirty minutes away, and he would need to stay there for two weeks. Also, because he had to have tubes in his chest, nobody would be able to hold him until he stabilized.

This sent me into turbo mama-bear mode. When they finally took the tubes out of his chest, five days into his stay in the NICU, I was insistent from the first moment that he get all the cuddles he missed out on during his first week of life. I set up revolving shifts of family to hold him constantly—like, all the time. Sure enough, his condition improved markedly as soon as he started getting wrapped in the arms of people who loved him.

The only problem was the night.

We now had my dad's help, since he had recently retired and moved to the area. Between him, Joe, me, and our moms, we could have someone with the baby pretty much all day. But there were seven hours at night when our son would be alone. Nobody could take the night shift since we were all so maxed out trying to keep things afloat with the five kids at home. The nurses often had to do procedures during that time, and they were usually so busy that they couldn't hold the baby afterward. The thought that my son could spend hours each night crying, alone, filled me with a despair so potent that it turned everything within me numb.

On the seventh day of the NICU stay, I arrived in the morning to see that Joseph had a new IV line in his scalp. When I asked a nurse about it, she explained the IV in his arm wasn't working, so they'd had to insert a needle into his head around three o'clock in the morning.

I pulled him close and sunk into the chair we kept next to his bed. I couldn't even think about my tiny son being scared and alone with no one to hold him after such a painful procedure. Since he wasn't premature, he was alert enough to have an awareness of what was going on. I imagined his eyes darting around, looking for someone to comfort him, and finding no one. I felt ill as I tried to push the thoughts from my mind.

My phone rang, showing my dad's number.

"How's the little guy doing?" he asked.

"Well. He has this IV in his head now."

"I know—and boy was he mad about that! He had a lot to say to those nurses who put that thing in."

"Wait . . ." my voice was distorted as my throat tightened. "What do you mean? You were there?"

"Yeah. I told you I'd stay."

My dad had developed a habit of making the forty-minute drive from his house to the hospital at midnight to walk my mom, his ex-wife, to her car after her baby-holding shift ended. He'd mentioned that he'd hang out with the baby for a bit afterwards, but I thought it was just a polite, passing comment. He was normally in bed by nine o'clock, so I figured he'd need to get home. "How long were you there?" I asked.

"I've been staying from the time I get there at midnight until they kick me out for the nursing shift change at six in the morning."

"You've been staying with him all night?"

"Sure have! Every night. He's my little buddy now."

I was literally speechless—my mouth was open, but I could not produce a single word. Eventually I managed to stammer out a thank-you and goodbye before I set down the phone to cry. Tears thick with relief and gratitude dropped onto the baby, and I kept having to use Joseph's blanket to dry him off.

When Joe and I made the decision to put down roots in this area despite the career sacrifices it would involve, we were following a vague sense that this was right for our family. As we sat at that Tex-Mex restaurant, under an elm tree, we were just doing our best to follow Fr. George's advice. Only now did I understand just what an invaluable gift we'd accepted when we made that choice.

Yaya now lived just a half mile away from us, having moved a few months before. After she saw that we were going to stay put for the long term, she sold her house of thirty years and relocated to be near us. The kids visited her at least a few days per week under normal circumstances and had been staying there for days on end during this current crisis. My mom still lived just a couple of miles from us, and she stopped by almost every day to drop a grocery item, to bring takeout on nights when I couldn't deal, or just to say hello. She'd been doing all of the kids' laundry since I was first diagnosed with the pulmonary embolisms, and, in a moment that left me dizzy with gratitude, she'd recently offered to keep doing it over the long-term. We regularly had the grandparents join us for dinner, the house filled with laughter and chatter and the smells of freshly cooked food.

And then there was my dad. Since the day I was sent to the emergency room, he'd become the unofficial family chauffer. He drove the big kids to all of their activities and took Lucy and Kate to Mother's Day Out, dropping them off as well as taking them home again. He brought his camera with him wherever he went, and each night he sent us perfectly crafted emails that summarized his trips with the kids. His skills as a writer shone as he recounted all the little poignant and funny moments with his grandchildren, so much so that he now had increasing numbers of relatives and family friends asking to be included on his updates.

Since that night at the Tex-Mex restaurant, we thought that we were creating a family orchestra, so to speak, made up of Joe, me, and the kids. Now I saw that it was so much bigger than that. The call we'd been given was to welcome all the people God was sending into our lives, from our own children to the neighbor girls to our parents to our church community and to other people who were yet to come. And when I thought again of the crescendo of love I'd seen in the past few months, culminating with my dad's all-night visits to hold my son, I saw that what we created when we all got together was beautiful indeed.

My Real Life

ON OUR SECOND-TO-LAST DAY IN THE NICU, Joe showed up early for his shift to sit with the baby, carrying a FedEx envelope under his arm.

"What's that?" I asked.

He handed it to me with a sly grin. "Open it."

Moving a sleeping Joseph over to one arm, I used my other hand to pull a stack of papers from the envelope. The contract. This was my book contract.

"Can you believe it?" Joe said, speaking quietly so he didn't wake the baby. "Your book is really going to be published!"

I couldn't. I just stared at it like it was a hologram that might disappear.

"Go ahead and sign it!" Joe said. "You can put it in the mail when you get home."

I stood slowly and carefully, making sure that the various wires that were attached to Joseph didn't get caught on the chair. I handed the baby to Joe, grabbed the pen he kept in his shirt pocket, and searched for a flat place to set the papers.

I thought of the long, long days I'd spent in this place in the two weeks since the baby's birth. I was often here six to eight hours at a time, in a corner of the floor with no windows. The cries of the babies with whom we shared the floor were never-ending and seemed to come from everywhere at once.

And one of the main things that helped me get through it was reading. Each day, when I arrived, I prayed for every baby in the room, and for the families, and for Joseph, and for us. And then, with hours left to go in my watch, I read. With Joseph cradled in my arms, I powered through a five-hundred-page, swashbuckling saga about a Viking named Red Orm. The sounds of this room and all the gut-wrenching stories that played out within it faded away as I leapt into this fictional world set in middle-ages Europe. I could see the God's-eye view of an entire life played out and absorb all the lessons that came with it. When I swiped the last page on my e-reader, I felt filled up and satisfied, like after you finish a hearty meal.

Reading that book had saved my sanity during this trial. And now, with my contract securely in hand, I would take my own place as a practitioner of the sacred art of the written story.

I found a spot on the edge of the baby's bed and carefully penned my signature on the contract for the book deal I'd been waiting for my whole life. I had imagined signing this contract amid clinking wine glasses and candlelight at a nice restaurant. Never would I have pictured this moment occurring in a place like this. Yet it had the cleansing effect of washing away all the nonsense that doesn't matter and leaving me with a crisp, clear understanding of what does.

In the decades that I'd been dreaming about having a book published, I'd had moments of yearning for prestige and glamor. Like how every actor has secretly rehearsed an Academy Awards speech in front of the mirror, I had fantasized about glowing reviews in respected publications, and I had a few witty remarks all prepared for my appearance on *The Tonight Show*. Now, this hospital room and all of its miracles and horrors had brought me back to the original reason why I got into any of this, and all of the daydreams about awards or acclaim seemed so trivial in comparison.

I wanted to tell stories to relieve people's burdens. When I first started writing books back in grade school, it was my escape after long days where I was perpetually the last kid picked for the team in gym class, the one who sat alone at the lunch table. Even in my child's mind, I knew I wanted to channel my own pain and turn it into a blessing for someone else. Now, when I thought back on how that book I'd been reading helped me get through our stay here in the NICU, it felt like hallowed work to be able to do the same for someone else.

As I handed the contract back to Joe, I prayed that all the time and sacrifice I'd put into this project might be transformed into a blessing for someone else who was going through a difficult time. And if that prayer were answered, even if the book received no other acclaim—even if it didn't end up bringing in much income—I could say with the whole of my heart that it was all worth it.

The next day, our last before going home, the doctor stopped by to check on Joseph. She pulled up a chair to chat after the exam. She and I had developed a good rapport and often struck up friendly conversations about a variety of subjects.

"So," she began, somewhat hesitantly, after we'd been talking for a while. "Now that you have six kids, are you guys done?"

I said yes, since that was the short answer she was looking for. Not surprisingly, Joe and I had decided that this needed to be our last baby. Even though I was fairly certain that the twice-daily injections that had cured the pulmonary embolism would keep me safe through another pregnancy, we didn't want to risk it.

My doctors thought I was insane for continuing to use Natural Family Planning to avoid pregnancy, but it was the right decision for us. From a purely medical perspective, I still couldn't take any hormonal contraception because of my clotting disorder. Nothing else except sterilization had high enough effectiveness levels, and for various reasons that we'd thought a lot about, that wasn't what felt right for us.

As I'd often observed, NFP is more of an alternative lifestyle than it was merely another form of birth control, and it was a lifestyle we'd gotten used to. Even the challenging parts had brought us close together. Getting our practice of this method up to the level that it would be a reliable way to avoid pregnancy would mean a lot of sacrifice. (We'd already made jokes that it would probably be easier if Joe went to live at a monastery for a while.) But we were committed, and, despite the fact that our history indicated nothing of the sort, I was confident that we really would be able to avoid pregnancy over the long term.

But were we "done"? I didn't know how to answer the question accurately because I didn't think in those terms anymore. If the question were confined only to a speculation on the odds that I would give birth to another child, then it was easy to answer. But, usually, when people asked this question, they had a bigger lifestyle shift in mind. The doctor articulated this for me with her next remark: "It'll be nice to get your life back after all these years. All of those pregnancies and babies—I can't imagine!"

Without taking up her whole afternoon, I didn't know how to explain that I no longer saw some time of endless personal freedom on the horizon for me. As our parents aged, our roles would slowly reverse, until one day we would be taking care of them. Joe and I would, hopefully, help our kids with their own children. We'd already begun talking with my dad about assisting with Papaw's care.

I thought of that sense I had, from the earliest moments of my conversion, that Joe and I were meant to have a big family. Certainly we'd achieved that with six kids, but now I understood this calling to be something bigger than the number of children to whom I'd given birth. I saw that what had been stirring in my heart for all these years was, in its broadest sense, a calling to let go of my individualistic ways. I came into faith and into parenthood with a mindset that my existence was ultimately about me, and that the hallmark of a good life was being able to control everything to my own taste. I thought that intimate service to others was only something you do for a few years when the kids are young. Now I saw it as the very foundation of a rich, fulfilling life.

"I don't know that I'm ever going to get my life back," I said through a laugh. "What you're looking at? This *is* my life."

The Box

I WAS SITTING AT THE TABLE on a Wednesday afternoon, going over school lessons with the four big kids, Pammy playing in the living room and one-year-old baby Joseph asleep upstairs. We were interrupted by a knock at the door.

"New friends!" Pammy shouted hopefully as she bolted for the hallway. In recent months, she had de-crazied a lot, and we were beginning to get glimpses of the kind, deeply empathetic young woman it seemed that she would become. She loved meeting new people, often taking visitors by the hand and asking to sit on their laps. Therefore, she always wanted it to be her job to get the door. We still had moments like a recent trip to the store where she screamed so violently about needing her window open that I thought a wasp must be attacking her; then, when I opened it, she cheerfully threw one of her shoes onto the street, that having been her goal all along. But those moments were becoming fewer, with more space between each one, and I saw her starting to channel her astounding energy and force of will toward taking care of the people she loved.

Pammy opened the door to reveal Carmen, Riley, and Megan, who were struggling with a large shipping box.

"Miss Jennifer, what *is* this?" Carmen said as she let it drop back onto the ground. "We were going to bring it in for you but I don't know if we can!"

"Did you, like, order a box of gold or something?" Megan wondered.

"I have no idea," I said. The return address label provided no clues. With the girls pushing and me pulling, we managed to get the box into the house, where Lane had already appeared with scissors. I dragged the blade along the tape at the top, and the girls pried the flaps open.

My books.

It was a box full of my books.

I jumped in the air as if someone had hit an eject button under me, and I screamed and babbled and generally made a complete fool of myself. I had expected them months from now. Seeing your first book in print is a moment you want to prepare for, and it was a glorious sensory overload to be caught off guard by this experience. I picked one up off the stack. It was hard to believe that this delicately bound, hardcover volume contained the Word document from my computer. I held it in my hand as if it were a sacred object. I even smelled it, which made the girls giggle. I ran my hands over the cover, then flipped to the back to see the author photo, a picture of me that Joe had taken with my phone.

I announced that we were having an impromptu celebration. I told Donnell and Lane to get the ice cream out of the freezer and asked Lucy to turn on some music. Pammy took Megan by the hands and started yanking her across the room as part of a dance she made up. Donnell practiced his drum work by slapping his hands on the table to the beat of the music, and Lane, Lucy, and Kate swirled around Carmen and Riley as they showed off their best ballet moves. It was four o'clock on an ordinary Wednesday afternoon and there were ten people in the house. Now that I thought about it, every day these days kind of felt like a party.

The next afternoon, I brought Papaw his copy of the book. Papaw was always my biggest cheerleader when it came to my writing. I'd given him a novel I'd written in fifth grade, and he read the entire thing like it was a John Grisham bestseller. He pored over the twelve-page description of the rituals of the secret club for popular kids and reported that he was "fascinated, just fascinated" by the plot line in which a girl who had a suspicious resemblance to me became the president of this exclusive club. He read lines like, *"That's the most rad perm ever," the head cheerleader said to Janny*, and reacted as if he'd been handed a previously undiscovered work of Shakespeare.

The whole family was there for a dinner to celebrate the book, the kids' ages now ranging from ten down to one. This time, my dad did the cooking; Papaw was now just shy of his one hundredth birthday, and he wasn't able to do much in the kitchen anymore. The kids flooded into his living room, and, as usual, his face beamed with delight. I waited for the commotion to settle down, then pulled up a chair next to him to present him with the surprise. I handed him the book and asked him to turn to the inscription, just before the title page. It read:

> *To Papaw, who always believed*

It was a double reference to the facts that he'd always had spiritual beliefs, and that he'd always believed in me.

He reached out to me to touch my arm, his hand cold and fragile. He couldn't seem to find the words. Finally, he said, his voice cracking, "You have no idea what this means to me."

We all knew that Papaw didn't have much time left. In addition to the whole almost-being-one-hundred thing, he'd been diagnosed with melanoma. It was a matter of months, not years. Maybe even weeks. I would forever be grateful that I was able to present my grandfather with the first copy of my book that I'd given to anyone. He'd been able to see his name, and only his name, on the dedication page.

If I had waited to write this story, Papaw would not have lived to see this. As I watched my aging grandfather stare at my book with tears in his eyes, I thought again of those messages that attack women, from both within and without, that whisper that we shouldn't pursue our dreams because we're not talented enough or we're too old or too young or we don't have the perfect lives for it. It occurred to me now that when we let Resistance hold us back, we're not the only ones who suffer. Other people lose out, too.

Release

"THEY WANT TO DO AN INTERVIEW TODAY?" I asked the PR rep for my publisher, who had called to tell me about a radio show that wanted to talk to me. I looked at the box of books on the floor next to my desk as we talked. Even though it had been sitting there for two weeks now, I still couldn't get used to that sight.

"They had a space open up at four o'clock. Are you free? It would be a long interview, but it's a great opportunity." The call waiting beeped, interrupting his words.

"Yeah, I think so—hang on. Let me see who this is."

I clicked to the other line to hear Yaya's voice. "Jennifer! I've got this so-called cough medicine here, some herbal thing I saw on a Judge Mathis ad that's supposed to have a bunch of flowers and weeds in it. I paid five ninety-nine plus shipping and it is useless! Do you have any real medicine over there at your house?" She seemed to be about to say something else but went into a coughing fit.

"Are you sick?"

"Yeah, I got this cold from Carlos over there on Timberline when he and Roger came over to help me get the internet on my email. I told him that he was going to get me sick!"

As usual, I had no idea who these people were, but I got her drift. She sounded terrible—and the fact that she admitted to feeling unwell at all caught my attention. When we were at her house a few days before, Kate had become scared by a wasp that landed on the chair next to her. Yaya grabbed the wasp, crushed it in her first, and threw it on the ground without interrupting her conversation. When I asked her if it stung her, she glanced at the red welt on her hand and shrugged. So if she said she didn't feel well, she must be absolutely miserable. "I think you should see a doctor."

"Yeah, I've got an appointment for four o'clock, but I don't know if I'm going to make it over. I don't think I can drive—I feel that bad."

"Let us drive you. And I'll go to the store and get you some good cough medicine, too. I'll pick up chicken soup while we're there." She started to protest, but I insisted. She finally relented, and I could hear the relief in her voice. Then I remembered the PR guy on the other line. I clicked back over.

"Sorry, I'm not going to be able to take that interview today."

"Jen, are you sure? They have a huge audience."

"Tell them I'd love to do it sometime, but today just doesn't work. I have another commitment."

I hung up the phone, called the kids to get ready, and grabbed my purse. The big kids helped the little kids into the car while I ran a brush through my hair and put on a swipe of lip gloss. When I took my place in the driver's seat, everyone was ready to go. We still didn't have a vehicle that fit our whole family, but with only one parent we could just barely fit everyone.

One thing that made it easier to get out the door was that I was already dressed to leave the house. I'd recently invested in fitted jeans and a half dozen light, summer cardigans in a variety of colors. Jeans with a black t-shirt topped by a colorful cardigan had become my standard daily uniform and actually made me feel half-way pulled together; it was also easy to change a top or a bottom when, say, a kid walked up and wiped their chocolate-smeared mouth on my clothes, as had happened this morning.

As soon as the car pulled to a stop in front of the store, I heard from the back seat: "Mommy, I don't have shoes!"

"Neither do I!"

This happened so often that I'd started to think of shoes as optional accessories. In fact, I had a plan all ready to deal with it.

The two barefoot ones, Lucy and Donnell, weren't allowed to walk on the store floor, so I had Donnell sit in the main part of the cart. I was going to stuff Lucy in there with him, but she insisted on riding in the very bottom overflow rack, where people usually put economy boxes of cat litter and toilet paper. Pammy and Joseph sat in the seat facing me up front, and Kate and Lane hung off the sides.

"You guys ready?" I said with a grin. They all shouted rowdy agreement, and Pammy began hopping up and down like she was on a bucking bronco. "Let's go!"

I ran the cart toward the store, the kids weighing it down enough that I could lean onto it and ride on the handles down a hill. I got the chicken soup for Yaya, since I'd learned that I had to get the most important thing first, even if it meant zigzagging across the store. Next we went for the cough medicine, speeding through the aisles, the kids cavorting in the cart like a band of merrymaking pirates.

I also picked up a few last-minute items for a dinner we were hosting the next night. We'd recently met a new family at our church, and we'd invited them and their four kids to join us for a meal. There was a time when cooking for fourteen people, ten of them children, would have overwhelmed me to the point that Joe would have come home to find me collapsed and twitching on the pantry floor. Now it didn't seem like that big of a deal. I had some hot dogs and burgers to throw on the grill, and I used this trip to pick up an economy size bag of frozen French fries. I'd even created a playlist for the occasion; it actually sounded great to me to have a house full of people.

We swung into an aisle and almost ran into a woman browsing the tea selection. She startled and looked up at us, then startled again when she saw my cart full of children. She was an elegant woman with perfectly sleek hair, and our interaction (mainly, the look on her face) immediately reminded me of my encounter with Green Bean Lady the day Donnell fell out of the cart so many years before.

She turned to stare at this traveling carnival that had almost run her over like roadkill.

"We're sorry!" Kate said, still at an age where her *r*'s sounded like *w*'s.

The woman's stunned gaze drifted down to the bottom of the grocery cart, and her face contorted into confusion when she saw Lucy wave at her from the bottom rack. She looked back up at me in want of an explanation.

"They had kids on sale today. Bought too many again!" I said and lurched the cart forward to begin a run down the aisle. I could feel her eyes on me as I jumped up on the handle to ride the cart, the kids shouting and cheering me on.

At checkout, I saw with dread that the cashiers were handing out balloons. They did this occasionally as a goodwill gesture toward their customers. I hated it every time since I had a fear of balloons popping that was as strong as it was irrational. I had too much pride to admit that I was a grown woman who was afraid of floating children's toys, so I always tried to come up with new and more creative excuses to get out of the store without them.

After he handed me the receipt, the checker turned to the stand behind him. He swirled back around holding six balloons in vivid primary colors. The kids were like mad hyenas as they tried to jump out of the cart and across the cash register to get their hands on the floating orbs of joy.

"Sorry, no balloons," I said. "The kids are afraid."

The checker looked at my children, whose actions were reminiscent of the crowds in old footage of Beetles concerts, and then back to me.

"They have a jubilant way of expressing their terror," I explained.

"BALLLLOOOOON!" Pammy shouted in her 115-decibel way. It was clear to the checker, to me, and to everyone within a mile radius who was going to win this one.

Out in the parking lot, six balloons bouncing in my face, I told the kids we couldn't take them home. Me in a car packed with balloons would be like a normal person being shoved into a wall locker packed with snakes—and being expected to drive the wall locker home.

"Let's let them go before we get in the car. You can make a wish on your balloon, then let it carry your wish to heaven!" I said, relying on the theological concept that God is more likely to answer prayers that are attached to rubber, helium-filled objects.

"Since you don't have a balloon, you can put your wish on mine," Lucy said.

"Yeah, what's your wish, Mom?" Donnell asked.

"Good question," I said. I tried to conjure up something to wish for, but I kept coming up empty. There were plenty of things I might want, but, at that moment, they were all dwarfed by an overpowering sense of gratitude for this crazy and beautiful life I was living. If these balloons were to symbolize messages we were sending up to God, the only one I could think of right now was simply: "Thanks."

We started a countdown and shouted the final numbers together. When we reached "one," the kids threw their hands in the air with squeals of happiness. I pulled them close, each one of us smiling as we watched the colors disappear into the sky.

Want to keep up with the
Fulwiler Family?
See the latest updates at

OneBeautifulDream.com!

Acknowledgments

Joe, thanks for always inspiring our family to live a great story.

Kids, you blow me away. Donnell, you are so wonderfully crazy and intense; Lane, I love your thoughtful, creative spirit; Lucy, you're my extrovert seeing eye dog; Kate, you've lifted me up on so many days with a saint story or just a hug; Pammy, I am so inspired by your deep concern for others; JT, you're my precious little guy (and I'm speaking in baby talk as I write that). I thank God every day for each one of you.

Mom (Pam Bishop), Dad (Don Bishop), and Yaya (Lou Fulwiler), it would take me one hundred pages even to list everything that you all do for us, then another hundred to express my thanks for it all. You know I'm not exaggerating when I say that, quite literally, this book would not exist without your generosity.

Lisa Jackson, I think of you more like a fairy godmother than a literary agent. I would still be staring at a blank document and muttering angrily if it weren't for your encouragement and sage advice.

I had highly unrealistic hopes for an editor for this project. Like my six-year-old asking Santa for a pony and a backyard water park, I dreamed of someone who would be brilliant, insightful, fun, understanding, and could nail editorial feedback from the thematic down to the sentence level. Stephanie Smith, you are all that and more.

Tom Dean, Curt Diepenhorst, Bob Hudson, Rebecca Jen, Alicia Kasen, David Morris, and the entire Zondervan team: You've created an environment where faith, kindness, and the pursuit of excellence all go hand-in-hand. I am so grateful to be a part of it.

Liz Aiello, Adam Hamway, Jackie Resciniti, and Joe Zwilling of SiriusXM / The Catholic Channel, thanks for being endlessly supportive as I figured out how to balance book writing with my radio job, and thanks for nodding politely when I say things like, "I think I'll try battle rapping on the show today."

Mark Brumley, Fr. Joseph Fessio, Eva Muntean, Anthony Ryan, and everyone else at Ignatius Press: Many of the books that most changed my life have the Ignatius name on their spines. It is an honor to be listed among your authors.

Nora McInerny said that "behind every great woman is another great woman replying to her frantic texts in the middle of the night." Everyone needs a friend like that; Hallie Lord, my Edel Gathering cofounder, thanks for being mine. Let's keep getting ourselves in over our heads with big ideas that ruin our lives.

Melanie Shankle, I am so lucky to have a foreword writer who is not only a friend but also one of my favorite authors.

Lino Rulli, thanks in advance for plugging this book on your radio show every day for a year. (You're going to do that, right?)

Charlene Sumlin, you gave me a boost exactly when I needed it. You knew when to send prayers and when to send prayers *and* a framed Geto Boys quote.

Ted Weinstein, thank you for believing that I could create something better than the garbage I kept sending you. You set a standard that I'll carry with me for the rest of my days as a writer.

Shady Ray Trejo, our house would have fallen apart a long time ago without your assistance.

To my radio listeners, my Edel Gathering ladies, and all of my friends from the online world: Know that your presence and your support mean more to me than I can express. I promise to keep telling nacho skirt stories for your entertainment.

To friends who read early drafts of this manuscript: Jewels Green, Kelly Mantoan, Stephanie Sullivan, Arwen Tibaldi, and Lisa Whitney, your feedback was invaluable. Jane Rosenman, once again, I would have been lost without your insights.

Frank and Patti Scofield, thank you for the kindness and generosity you've shown our family over the years.

Gabi, Marlena, Raegan, and Valerie, you guys were a light in my life during a really chaotic season, and it's been a delight to see the lovely young women you've become. You can ring my doorbell any time.

And thank you, Jesus, for always being there, even when I didn't realize it. All beautiful dreams begin with you.